P9-APL-172

Lorette Wilmot Library
Nazareth College of Rochester

DEMCO

WITHDRAWN

"BUT THEY WON'T TALK WITH A WOMAN"

The Processing of a Model for Confronting Justice Issues Between Female and Male Clergy

---

Leta Gorham
Thomas W. Waitschies

University Press of America,® Inc.
Lanham • New York • Oxford

WITHDRAWN
LORETTE WILMOT LIBRARY
NAZARETH COLLEGE

Copyright © 1998
University Press of America,® Inc.
4720 Boston Way
Lanham, Maryland 20706

12 Hid's Copse Rd.
Cummor Hill, Oxford OX2 9JJ

All rights reserved
Printed in the United States of America
British Library Cataloging in Publication Information Available

Library of Congress Cataloging-in-Publication Data

Gorham, Leta
But they won't talk with a woman : the processing of a model for
confronting justice issues between female and male clergy / Leta
Gorham, Thomas W. Waitschies.
p.   cm.
Includes bibliographical references.
l. Women clergy. 2. Sexism—Religious aspects—Christianity. 3.
Feminism—Religious aspects—Christianity. I. Waitschies, Thomas
W. II. Title.
BV676.G67   1998   262'.14'082 —dc21   98-5300 CIP

ISBN 0-7618-1046-3 (cloth: alk. ppr.)
ISBN 0-7618-1047-1 (pbk: alk. ppr.)

⊖™ The paper used in this publication meets the minimum
requirements of American National Standard for information
Sciences—Permanence of Paper for Printed Library Materials,
ANSI Z39.48—1984

262.14
Cor

A Journey With Jesus:
An effort to understand the intended relationship
between female and male proclaimers of the
Gospel in today's Church.

Contents

Note from the authors

It is our intention to continue our pattern of dialogue throughout the entirety of this paper. We have found, much to our delight, that this process enhances our own personal and spiritual growth. We will intersperse our dialogue throughout the remaining chapters of this work if and when it is appropriate rather than putting it at the end as we have done in this introduction.

We invite you to join us on this journey with the hope that God will lead you to stand with us in this struggle for justice.

Chapter One

A Journey into a New Liberation Movement

Leta's Journey

"He thinks that you don't respect him!" said my superintendent. "Hallelujah! Is that all?" I wanted to shout out loud. Here I was, faced with a cut in my salary of 50%, and I wanted to shout, "Hallelujah!" How could that be? Well, he did not say, "She's incompetent."-or-"She's not pastoral."-or-"She's lazy." All he said was, "He thinks that you don't respect him." [1]

No official took the time to check out the veracity of the charge. No one even bothered to ask either him or me to define "respect". Had I communicated lack of respect through conversation with him or through body language? The one who made the charge which would greatly affect my life and my career was the senior pastor of a large church, and that automatically meant that he was male. As a female who had to be moved to another place of ministry my experience told me that I could not even expect to receive a comparable paying appointment as my male predecessor had two years prior to this event, for he, having grown up in a patriarchal society and church system had known his "place". An intelligent female should have known her place, too. To "know one's place" is an extremely important element of communication in our patriarchal society, and I, as a female, had expected a bit of mutuality, a bit of sharing, a bit of serious theological dialogue, even a bit of camaraderie as the males on the staff shared. That translated itself into "lack of respect". Yet, I wanted to shout, "Hallelujah!" Crying would come later. For the moment, I needed to celebrate the fact that I was emotionally, and not just intellectually, a part of that group of women, sometimes called feminists, who affirm " the wholeness and worthiness of all humankind, and I was able to pose with meaning a question that I had claimed for myself through prayer long, long ago, "With whom do you want me to stand today, O God?"

For the first time in my life I knew anger as an offended woman. Previously, I had interpreted the feelings which I had experienced as a result of abusive situations in the church as ones of sadness and grief. Now there was no doubt that what was foremost in my mind and in my heart was anger that a male pastor with the support of a male hierarchy could so disrupt my life. And, yet I would never define myself as a radical feminist, because I have known the love and complete support of a man who would at any time have given up his position of power, if necessary, in order for me to experience wholeness.

As a Child Protective Services Specialist for 12 years, I often did parent training, geared primarily to parenting abused and neglected children. I often said to the parents, "Listen to and look closely at what your child is trying to say to you, and then choose your battle ground wisely. You cannot win them all. What is of vital importance to you? For what you choose must be that for which you are willing to give your life." Now I was ready to take my place beside those who struggled for the affirmation of women even if it meant my life and not just my job.

As a very young child, a preschooler, I was assigned to be the Bible reader to my great-grandmother who was losing her eyesight. Reading her Bible was the highlight of her day, so it became the highlight of my day as well. We chewed on the words and explored the stories in great depth, and Grandma taught me how to tell The Story by having me tell all the Bible stories back to her, a thing which she said, "Preachers can't do." I've tried to remember just how it all took place, but I have been unable to pinpoint any specific times. I do know that during that time together, I became what would later be called a liberation theologian and an activist in the cause of justice for all people. Or, so I thought, for I reasoned later on that women who were self-affirming or even women, in general, did not need liberating. This reasoning I now know, was a part of my cultural conditioning—a strong message that women receive by osmosis. [2]

Even way back then, I realized that I was different. Certain issues were important to me which were not important to my friends. Growing up in a small north Texas town where no one but a white "looking" person could let the sun set on him or her and where only Protestants were acceptable religious folk marked me for life. Both of my parents were ethnically Choctaw and Cherokee, but not visibly so, and thus very careful that my sister and I grew up respecting people of other races and other cultural backgrounds. When racist or ethnic jokes were told, even in family gatherings, my mother took us quietly out of the group. The first and only one of two occasions on which I saw my father cry involved a time when he had used a common racist term, one with which he had grown up, in front of an African-American co-worker and saw a look of pain pass briefly over his face. He was so very ashamed.

When I was about ten years of age, an uncle came home from World War II after having helped liberate a concentration camp. He was never emotionally stable again. Being a farmer, he would continue his work with little difficulty, for it gave him much time to be alone and with that which he loved and from which he drew strength. He married his long-time sweetheart but never had children. He would mutter to himself even in a crowd and jerk his head and act in a way that was considered bizarre by most people. He began to read to me and to help me to learn about the Jews, "who should never have been treated like that," according to my uncle. He had never met a Jew before that time. This was a life-changing experience for him and for me. He approached this learning/teaching experience with a passion, and I was a beneficiary of that passion.

During my senior year in high school a friend was expelled from school when she became pregnant. The father of the child, the captain of the football and basketball teams, was not. I continued to visit her to keep her "connected"—not knowing at the time what "connected" meant but knowing that it "felt" right. My friends all said that I could afford to do so only because I was a cheerleader. I thought even then that it was much more than that. It had to do with what I had been learning in Sunday School about the Christ and how we relate to others in love as we relate to a loving God.

There were other issues of which I now understand to be related to "justice" and "fairness" such as the way our town folks talked about Roman Catholics and the only divorced woman in our home town, and these caused me to ponder their ultimate meaning or perhaps my ultimate meaning as one human being called by God to fight for the rights of these people who were only marginally a part of my world until I went away at age 17 as a married student to Southern Methodist University. I was accompanying a young man who had asked me to go with him as a missionary teacher to Africa.

Our life in Dallas in the 50s was full of opportunities to become immersed in justice issues, and my husband and an African-American theology student were the first two to "do" a sit-in in downtown Dallas. I then led the first threatened move-out at Perkins School of Theology student housing where my husband and I were dorm directors. No African-American married students could live with us. From that time on life was full of opportunities to "stand beside the marginalized and the oppressed" not only in the United States but in

Europe and particularly in Kenya and Zaire, Africa, where we lived and worked for approximately 11 years. Somehow, when it came time "to stand", it was always very clear that God was there with me, and the cause was crystal clear. I took seriously the Scripture passage, "...you will come to know the truth, and the truth will set you free" (John 8:32NJB). I just knew that any "good" Christian who saw injustice anywhere would fight against it. And, now many years later, I was finding myself among the marginalized and the oppressed. Was it possible that God was telling me again with whom to stand? Was that person me?

I have tried to track my journey in the area of women's rights, and it is not easy. My mother was the first woman school bus driver in our home town, but that was acceptable during World War II. There was a place for women and a place for me as a woman in this world. I never considered it unusual that all ministers were male. That was just the way that it was. Even when I was a student at Perkins School of Theology the first time, doing my Master of Arts degree, it did not seem unusual that we had only one female divinity student who was a missionary and did not intend to seek ordination. I was most often the only female who dialogued with the male theologues, but I, too, was a "missionary", and that made it okay. The men gave me the impression that they thoroughly enjoyed including me in their discussions. It was not unusual in my mind that all the professors were male, for we all knew that theology was a male subject. But, I really did dig those theological discussions. My husband always included me in his theologizing. In fact, I was his closest confidant. He encouraged me to think of my presentations as "sermons" and not just "talks" when we traveled around as missionaries on furlough. Most always he was asked to preach, and we taught classes separately and then did a joint "dog and pony" show for evening presentations. There were times, however, when we would be in different churches on Sundays, and I would "preach" during the worship hour. They would introduce me as a speaker who was going to give a "talk;" whereas, my husband was always introduced as the preacher, and his was always a sermon.

We had intended to spend our lives in Zaire as missionary teachers, but the health and education of our children forced us to return to the United States. While overseas, I led protests against unfair transportation charges for Zaireans and against racist attitudes of missionaries. After three years as a French teacher in a university, my husband entered the pastoral ministry. He had been ordained 11 years prior to that time in Africa with absolutely no difficulty in the process. I never questioned that. It was during that time of serving in his first pastorate that he began to urge me to return to theology school and prepare myself for the ordained ministry in order to serve with him.

He recognized my call and gifts long before I. I was to be the preacher and he the pastor. Although I preached often, I could not get beyond the personal barrier of believing that ordained ministry was really for men. The few ordained women I knew were divorced women who were very angry with their former mates. They expended a great deal of energy telling their story and the stories of how they were treated or rather mistreated by male colleagues. Their anger scared me. I had been a very successful missionary teacher where all missionaries, male or female, doctor or teacher, made the same salary and were respected for what we did. I was a successful social worker where I made the same salary as my male colleagues and was the most respected social worker in our county in Court. I was very happily married and had absolutely no reason to be angry with my husband. Even though I served on the Conference Commission on the Status and Role of Women for three years — which meetings always left me feeling scared — I kept a wide berth from the feminists. When my husband asked a female parishioner to assist him in serving Holy Communion, I thought that he was going a bit far. I was not sure that it "would take". He never let up on urging me to go back to theology school. Then he died rather unexpectedly, and all the doors that he had made open for me to serve in the church closed almost immediately. I was no longer Jack's wife but a strong, self-affirming female, and it scared the male pastors with whom I interacted. Could it have been that they perceived me in a different light, a greater threat, since I no longer had a man to control me — to keep me in my place? [3]

In the process of grief therapy I realized that I had been called all my life to be in ordained ministry. I finally went to seminary. If I had been scared by the feminists before, I was terrified of them in seminary. I really did not like them. Their anger was overwhelming. I was experiencing deep grief over the loss of a loving mate of almost 35 years, and they were telling me how abusive men were! I was invited to take part in a worship service for women's week during my first year, and was uninvited when they "discovered" that I was not a feminist. There was never any discussion about the discovery of how the women found out or the change in the invitation. My closest friends and colleagues in seminary were males, but all my psychological testing to be a missionary or a pastor showed that I related much better to males than to females anyway, so that did not surprise me that they were my best friends. Then I discovered that the route through theology school and that which led to ordination were totally different journeys, and the loving atmosphere with my male colleagues in seminary was not evident in the male-dominated committees in the conference, with few exceptions, or with the male senior pastors with whom I served. There was never a doubt that when

I did something outstanding in worship or teaching to which both male
and female parishioners responded positively, the men supervising me
would become irritated about something I had done—maybe long ago
or even shortly before the successful event. [4]

My life-long commitment to the establishment of a loving
community kept me from giving up or actually admitting that I might
not be wrong all the time—that it just might be that the male pastors
with whom I directly related were threatened by me and that I would
have to accept the fact that I would be punished for being successful. I
would not give up my dream, however, that if I was caring enough and
submissive enough, I would be allowed to serve. Note, I used the
word "allowed", for I still thought as a female of my time where
women were subservient to men and where men decided who would
serve where. I kept looking for another male like my husband—maybe
even a protector as women of my generation were groomed to do. And
now I was being told that I must move from a ministry which I loved
and where I was loved, because, "He thinks that you don't respect
him." And, I was saying, "Hallelujah!" for I had finally embraced the
journey.

I had never abandoned my query to God, "With whom do you want
me to stand today?" for I had recently stood beside the people with
AIDS and those who were gay. I would now stand beside myself
because my cause was just and who could understand the pain of being
oppressed as a woman better than I?

As I recently shared the above experience with my friend, Tom, and
told him how I had preached a sermon on the sacredness of the
creation of women two years ago to two Schools of Christian Mission
described with joy by many of my friends, some of whom were
feminists, as one only a "flaming liberal" could preach, I queried as to
why I could never embrace the women's movement until this final
incident—why not when I preached the sermon or taught the course?
"Why could I not then ask the Lord," 'With whom do you want me to
stand today?'" I queried. To this he replied, "Because this is the first
time that you have been called to stand beside yourself and not
necessarily beside someone else."

I am ready now to begin this journey as it leads to justice and
affirmation of all God's creation, even of women, and I am convinced
that it has a lot to do with how males and females communicate and
use power over one another and how the local church congregations
communicate the value they place on a male and female pastor. This is
rooted in our long history of a paternalistic society in which "...in
every sector..., women were in a subordinate position, the Church was
one of the most dominant forces for maintaining them in this position."
5

We have the whole biblical history of men in charge and the Holy Family where Joseph is head of the household and was not even the biological father of Jesus. To depart from this model entails for a woman, "...threats of violence..." [6] where women know that they will suffer through their salary and loss of position. We refer to the church congregation as a family which implies that the father is the head. In a recent meeting in which Tom and I were present a female associate to a male senior pastor explained how the congregation viewed them. He was seen as "Daddy" and she as "Mommy," and she said that she saw this as totally appropriate. She also said that she knew that there wasn't even the slightest possibility that she would ever be considered for "Daddy's" position and his much larger salary.

Turning my journey from the emotional to the intellectual has been difficult, but because of this requirement, I am much better able to make a journey which will help not only me, but my sisters and brothers in ministry.

Tom's Journey

My understanding of justice began almost at the moment that I was born. At birth I was abandoned by a mother who either did not want me, or could not keep me. However, God's grace provided for me two parents who had much love to share with a child, any child, even an abandoned child. I carry with me an understanding of what it means to be a stranger at the gates, hoping that someone will notice you and take pity on you.

I was raised in the Missouri Synod Lutheran Church, and it was there that I began my journey of faith. I was taught the stories of the Bible, where God sided with those who were oppressed—the widows, the orphans and the strangers. I listened intently as Jesus confronted situations of oppression and injustice. It always seemed to me that Jesus was saying to all of his followers that to love God was to love one's neighbor. As Jesus illustrated in his parable of "The Good Samaritan", one's neighbor very likely is someone who may be very different from one's self.

In the church in which I had grown up, the same church which had taught me what it meant to be a follower of Christ, I was confronted with a terrible contradiction. During the regular worship service on a Sunday morning an African-American couple came in the door of the church. The ushers were at their posts, everyone was seated, the pastor was leading the service, and no one seemed to take notice of the couple who stood at the back of the church waiting to be seated. The usher closest to them looked at them when they came in the door, but he didn't speak and he didn't offer to show the couple to a seat. If the people in the church would treat these people this way, did that mean that God didn't love these people? Had I missed something? Were there options as to whom I could be kind and to whom I could be unkind?

It was when I was in elementary school that the desegregation order was carried out in the public schools in my home town. My parents placed my brother and me in a private school to avoid our attending an integrated school. I still did not understand why African-Americans were not welcome. It was true that they looked different from me. It was true that they talked and acted differently than I did. But didn't God create them just like God created me? Wasn't God concerned with providing for them just as God had provided for me? My parents were not able to easily afford the tuition at the private school, and so the day came when I was finally going to go to school with African-American children. What I quickly found out was that my parents and others were right. African-Americans were different from me! Their skin was a different color. Their hair was a different texture. Even their way of expressing themselves was different. However, the qualities that were the same between me and them far outnumbered the differences. They laughed just like I did. They cried just like I did. They felt pain just like I did. And their parents loved them just like mine loved me.

When I was in high school, I found that I was in the minority. The high school which I attended was approximately 91% African-American. There is a different feeling being in the minority. Some would say the feeling is fear. Others would say there is a feeling of having to be cautious not to offend those who are in the majority. Still others would say that there is an unidentifiable feeling of uncomfortableness. I'm not sure why, but I never felt uncomfortable in a situation where I was in the minority. I suppose part of the reason is that the environment was not hostile, and another part of the reason was that no one was aggressively trying to oppress me. As I reflect upon that experience, I would have to say that a large contributing factor to my feeling comfortable in such a situation may have to do with my early experience of, to coin a phrase from A Streetcar Named Desire, having to depend "on the kindness of strangers." In addition to my own experiences and reflections, an unnamed African-American friend gave me another clue. He said the reason that African-Americans are not as uncomfortable in arenas where they are the minority stems from their "having grown up having to live and fit into two cultures." This situation accustomed African-Americans to being in the minority much of the time.

As I grew into adulthood, I wandered away from the church, because there were too many contradictions between what was professed and what was practiced. I traveled around and worked at a few different jobs before I ended up in a town in West Texas. It was there that I met a young African-American man who got me interested in the Church again. He was the pastor of a small African-American United Methodist Church, and he invited me to come to his church. I told him that I would come sometime but that I had never been to an African-American church and would like to know what it would be like? As I vascilated on whether or not to go, he continued to invite me, and he wouldn't take "No" for an answer. Finally, I relented. It was a strange moment for me to experience worship in the context of an African-American setting. I had gone to school with African-Americans, and I had been very close friends with African-Americans, but this was the first time that I had experienced another culture at its deepest level. It seems to me the ways which we experience and worship God strike at the deepest level of our cultural awareness. It is in that moment of being in the presence of God that all of whom we are is exposed. That day I felt the presence of God like at no other time in my life. I could not pinpoint exactly what made this experience different except that these people, these African-American brothers and sisters of mine, expressed God's love to me by accepting and welcoming me. I wasn't welcomed and accepted because I was white or black, rich or poor, but I was welcomed and accepted because I was a child of God. Once again I was in the presence of a loving God who, through these people, continued to love and care for me as I was a stranger in a strange land.

I had been affected by what I witnessed as a child in the way of white people's behavior toward African-Americans. I felt ashamed of what my race had done to people of another race and what was still occurring to African-Americans because of their color, but their battle had not been my battle. I felt a kinship to abandoned and orphaned children, because that was my battle. But now that I had experienced the Holy Presence through the culture of my African-American brothers and sisters, their battle against injustice became my battle. The fire for justice was stoked and my resolve to make the issue of justice for African-Americans my issue was forged in that moment. No longer could I turn a deaf ear to the problems assailing my African-American sisters and brothers, for their problems were my problems. I identified their struggle for justice as a struggle of which I needed to be a part. Here were a people who were much like me. They, too, were at the gate as a stranger, hoping to be given equal status by the gatekeepers. They, too, were strangers in a strange land.

Not long after that time, I moved to a major metropolitan area and joined an African-American United Methodist Church. I became involved in the life of that church and of my fellow parishioners. The members of my home church included me in every facet of the church's life. I was asked to sing in the choir. I was invited to a Sunday School class and later was asked to teach that class. I was asked to be a member of the United Methodist Men's group and later was asked to serve as their president. So it was not that I was a token white person in this sea of African-Americans; rather, they had made me one of their own. It was remarked more than once that they often forgot that I was white. Some would say that was a devaluing of who I was as a person; however, I took it as a sign that they loved and respected me for who I was, not for what I was.

It was in that setting that I began to feel God's call upon my life to enter the ordained ministry. The members of my home church felt a sense of pride and ownership in that call. They knew that they were the reason that I was able to get in touch with my call. They also knew that I would forever remember from where I came. I began the process toward ordained ministry, and when I finished my undergraduate work, I entered seminary. While in seminary, I felt a constant barrage of justice issues that confronted different racial groups as well as gender groups. I paid close attention to some of the feminist issues but felt called to continue my focus on justice issues as they related to African-Americans.

After I was graduated from seminary, I was in an assigned group where several female clergy were present. In the course of our discussions, issues of justice concerning the female clergy were brought to light. It was in this assigned group that I got to know Leta, and when she was accepted to the Doctor of Ministry program at Perkins, I decided to enter the program at the same time. There was a sort of kindred spirit that I sensed in Leta, not knowing at the time that a large part of that kindred spirit had to do with the struggle for justice and equality.

During our class work in this program we have again touched on issues of justice as it relates to female clergy. It has been during this time that my consciousness has been raised to the level that I became aware of the seriousness of the issue of justice as it relates to female clergy. How can one group of people exclude another group when God calls on God's people to stand with the orphan, the widow, and the alien? Anyone who stands outside the gate of acceptability has been given protection by God, through God's people. Certainly, in the Church where women are systematically excluded from the positions of power and treated unjustly, God's people need to be taking a long, hard look at where they stand.

When Leta decided to do her project on justice issues as it relates to differing styles of communication between male and female clergy, I asked if it would be possible for us to do a joint project; whereby, we would confront this issue from both gender perspectives. It is my belief that those who are oppressed must stand and fight for what is right, but it also takes at least some of those who are among the oppressors standing with the oppressed in order to bring about change. As Leta and I have begun to form a partnership with one another, I feel myself again standing with those who are strangers in a strange land.

Leta and Tom's Dialogue

Since the theme of our Project is communication between female and male clergy, it seems appropriate that we model this method ourselves by dialoguing throughout a portion of our Project. Granted, we have less disagreement than what may be normally observed between clergy colleagues or we would not have undertaken the Project together. It would be our hope, however, that as clergy begin to explore these issues, they will find that as children of God and models of Christ, we have more in common than we have that divides us.

Tom: You said that you "expected a bit of mutuality" from the senior pastor when you worked on a large church staff. Did you also expect some of that mutuality from the denominational system of appointment? And if so, what kept you from demanding more equitable treatment than your past counterparts had received?

Leta: Yes, I did expect "a bit of mutuality" in the denominational system of appointment, and because of that expectation, I did not go forward and demand equal treatment. I realize that I may be confusing "mutuality" with "trust." Because I had felt that I was being listened to and because I had been assured of support by my male supervisors, which actions I interpreted to be signs of mutuality, I trusted that they would do what they had said that they would do. I greatly underestimated the power of the male dominated hierarchical system which does not include women to any significant degree. I believe that this is a sub-conscious action, rather than an intentional one, a product of growing up in our society. I expect/ed the ministers of the Church to be intentional. I expect/ed them to be different from the person on the street.

Tom: Isn't trust a female characteristic? I don't believe that males trust any system, even that of the Church. We learn how to work the system; whereas, women learn a different way of relating.

Leta: As to the second part of your question, I think that I just presupposed that I would be treated with justice. It was an extreme hurt for me to realize that, not only was I not treated justly but I was not paid justly. As an added thought, I believe that males and females even view justice differently. I not only did not understand the system sufficiently but believed that even if it existed in society, it would not exist in the Church where we preach justice. Using power to demand justice for myself was/and perhaps still is, a difficult concept for me to embrace. Further, I must ask, "In our system, do I have any power to use?" Gillespie says in a discussion of power that in a family or in society in general power is not based on "...individual resources or personal competence of the partners..." because "...women are blocked as a class, not as individuals." [7] She maintains that egalitarianism is a myth and not a norm.

There is another aspect of this situation. Jean Baker Miller brought out my understanding and my feelings about what took place when she pointed out the "rules of the game" as presented to her by C. Gilligan. I quote, *...one learns that it is the game that counts, not the people or the personal relationships among them. Trying to beat the other, hitting as hard as you can, and the like does not mean you are hurting anyone personally; you are just playing the game. Likewise, the recipient should not take it personally; it does not really hurt. But as far as I can see, it does. Clinical work with men reveals that it hurts in many ways.*

Then, as the game is carried over into adult life, it allows men to compete, win, drive out the opposition, even totally destroy them. The game is played with the pretense that no one really is hurt. .... [8]

And, I found that not only did I not know the rules of the game, but I really did hurt.

Tom: To follow up on this, you said in your story that you reasoned fairly early on as you became involved in justice/liberation issues that women didn't need liberating. How did you come about such an opinion?

Leta: Many women, particularly those with whom I am closely related, were as comfortable in their role as subservient homemaker as men were in their power role. The generation with which I am related felt secure in having men to protect us, not only physically but also in the simple business of balancing checkbooks, taking the car to the shop where mechanics not only used vulgar language from which women were to be protected but who also presupposed that women did not understand mechanical things and would humiliate women. There were also matters such as repairing the commode, accepting the full responsibility for support of the family along with numerous other issues which denote power and protection versus dependence and insecurity. In fact, it was only after I made my entrance into the feminist movement, that I began to meet women who adamantly refused to discuss being liberated if it took away their sense of security or of feeling protected.

Tom: Before we leave this issue of justice, I would like to pick up on your idea that males and females see justice from a different perspective. As I think about it, I believe that justice for men translates itself into money and power. For women, respect and support are more important issues of justice. In the end, however, by holding these as primary attributes, women lose money and the power that goes with money.

Leta: We need to explore this further, because we have both seen how this is played out in the Church.

Tom: I have found this to be true of all oppressed groups. For example, the house slaves who were more humanely treated than the field slaves often chose dependency and protection over liberation. Those who initiate the fight for liberation appear to be those who feel pain the most deeply, whether mental or physical.

Tom: I'd like to discuss further your idea of "connected" as you used it in your story about the high school friend who became pregnant.

Leta: As I've read more and more about women's issues, I have learned that "being connected" is a very important form of support for women. I believe that women do not desire to be at the top of a hierarchy if that means being alone. We now understand that if we don't struggle to get to the top, we will be punished economically and will not be listened to in the same way as those who are at the top who are usually men. Personally, I did not want my friend to be alone because I function best in community and worse when I am alone, and it was unjust to see her withdrawn from the group and the father of the child still connected. I see now that "connection" was not what was important to him but rather staying in the power structure was.

Tom: As a pastoral person I find that I draw strength from helping other people stay connected. It is not necessarily as important to help the other person stay connected as it is to help me experience wholeness. I think that is what you are saying about the fact that you function best in community. That is an acceptable trait for women but not necessarily for men. Men see it as a weakness if you can't stand alone.

Leta: You've just related your understanding of a feminist "feeling" and you spoke about becoming aware of feminist issues in a group we once shared. Could you tell me a little bit more about specific events or things that happened to cause this awareness?

Tom: In the beginning I was turned off by the abundance of complaints about relationships between male senior pastors with female associates. I grew tired of hearing it. I cannot tell you exactly what changed my mind or opened my awareness, but I do believe somehow that the Holy Spirit opened me to the pain rather than to the actual story. One day I realized that it wasn't just one female's story but the stories of all the females in the group who were at different stages of maturity in life and service to the Church and yet who were all experiencing humiliation in the Church's system. They had different ways of expressing anger which at first I had interpreted to be fear, sadness, complacency and actual pathos. Then one day I said to myself, "This is not a group of angry women. This is a matter of justice being denied to all persons without power." A lot of it seemed to stem simply from different ways that the female and male clergy went about ministry and communicated with one another and to their congregations.

Leta: I sense that there were times that you were really turned off by the conversations in the group. What kind of action did this cause you to take?

Tom: I really thought about withdrawing mentally from the conversation, just enduring the three hours that we were forced to spend together. Something inside me, perhaps my personal relationship to you and your struggles as a female in ministry, caused me to be more intentional in observing male/female relationships and in reading to expand my understanding of the issues involved. One article in particular comes to mind. Clarence Page, a columnist for the Chicago Tribune, speaks about how those of power want to solve all problems without discussion; whereas, the powerless want to discuss the issues involved in the problem. The latter attitude involves concern for people and relationships. As I started out in the group, I just thought, "Well, heck, why don't you women just go confront those male pastors and say, 'We just won't tolerate this!' Then we can get on to what's important in our group." Later, I realized that that couldn't take place because of the system but also that the women were more interested in telling their story and being heard than they were in being told what to do about it.

Leta: I was turned off at times, too, at hearing the stories over and over, but I was more concerned that the other women were angry when they told their story. This scared me. As I thought about it, I realized that I have always been scared of anger, and it was a call to me to get beyond that fear in order to listen and to respond to the pain that was being presented.

Tom: Did you ever begin to feel that the anger expressed by the women was well-founded?

Leta: I really got in touch with that when I realized that I was becoming a victim of the system. I first saw myself as sad and finally realized that I was very angry. I had always tried to respect the system because I had been taught that it was of God, and I found that respect was not an appropriate reaction to the misuse of power.

Tom: Given that we both have come to the conclusion that women are not treated fairly, is anger the emotion that is most appropriate to feel? If so, how do we direct the anger?

Leta: At this point in time, I would say that anger is the only possible feeling. Later, we must move on and out of anger in order to work toward justice. We cannot remain stuck in anger.

Tom: You speak of knowing what was right and what was wrong even in your childhood and I speak of questioning why what I learned in Church was not what I saw acted-out by the church members. Have we learned anything from those experiences which will help us in this issue of how to create better communication between male and female clergy resulting in justice for all?

Leta: To me justice is a theological issue and the foundation of all that we stand for and preach from our pulpits.

Tom: The issue of justice will be interesting as we struggle with it in our groups. I see justice as a theoretical issue, also because we need to find a way to solve the problem and stop the hurting. Your personal experience is one example of the ways that males and females say things differently or perhaps operate differently and end up separating themselves from one another.

Leta: You and I have both been involved in Civil Rights, African-American and other issues of liberation, and you specifically mentioned that you are ashamed of what the Church has done to African-Americans. Is shame an appropriate word to use when we talk about the oppression of female clergy? If so, will you use this in confronting male pastors with their misuse of power? If so, how will you do this?

Tom: As I think about this, I realize that shame will not motivate them to change. In fact, it might worsen the problem because it could cause them to hide their real feelings. Guilt, fear and anger are greater motivators for both the oppressor and the oppressed. I see our consciousness-raising groups as a tremendous tool for growth for all those who are involved.

Tom: In relating your story of your husband and your visiting churches to talk about your work in Africa, you have said that there was a distinction made between your "giving a talk," and your husband's "preaching a sermon." Are you sure that that distinction was drawn because you were a woman or because you were a lay person? If it was the former, why are you sure that the reason was your gender?

Leta: Your question points up a very important issue relating to my journey into the feminist movement. In fact, it embarrasses me. The reality is that I was a lay person, and I did give a talk. Despite my husband's urgings, I did not respond to the call to ordained ministry, but I considered myself in ministry, because I had been commissioned as a missionary. Once I answered the call and prepared myself for ordained ministry, I expected surely then to be treated as a fully ordained minister as were my male friends. I found that this was not true. Even after "paying my dues," I was still Leta; whereas, the male clergy on the staff where I served were Reverend or Doctor. As I prepared "my story," I fell prey to the tendency of the oppressed to name all slights or humiliations as sexist discriminations rather than accepting the fact that I was a lay person at the time mentioned. My efforts must be much more focused on affirmation of the rights and privileges of all ordained persons regardless of their sex.

Footnotes

N. B. Many of our footnotes will be handled in the following style, according to Kate L. Turabian pp. 123-124 #6: 155. The decision to do this is based on an effort not to interrupt the flow of the conversational style of this Project. Each footnote handled in this manner is a direct quote from the source.

1   Men, however give much more legitimacy to the entry of personal considerations into their decisions, and it feels all right to them when it involves issue of power, competitiveness, or even vindictiveness. I heard a man say recently that he was going to fire someone: "He does not accept my authority." Well, that is pretty personal--hardly a measure of the person's competence--yet he felt perfectly comfortable in thinking it was a perfectly good reason to fire an employee. Jordan, Judith V. and Kaplan, Alexandra G. and Miller, Jean Baker and Stiver, Irene R. and Surrey, Janet L., Women's Growth In Connection. (New York: The Guilford Press, 1991), p. 229.

2   By the mid-70's, the media and advertisers had settled on a line that served to neutralize and commercialize feminism at the same time. Women, the mass media seemed to have decided, were now equal and no longer seeking new rights--just new lifestyles. Faludi, Susan, Backlash (The Undeclared War Against American Women). (New York: Anchor Books, Doubleday, 1991) p. 76.

3   ...there is a strong reservoir of attitude on the part of the American male that he has a right to tell his wife what to do...In our society, the husband who successfully asserts his dominance does enjoy some approval and even a modicum of envy from other males. Male dominance is to some extent approved. Gillespie, Dair L., "Who Has the Power? The Marital Struggle," Journal of Marriage and the Family, (University of California, Berkley: August 1971) p. 453, and "Patriarchal culture senses danger in an unmarried woman. ...Mainly, it is that women are no one's property when we're unmarried. We're under no one's control, and neither are our children. There's no telling what we might do or say." Williamson, Marianne, A Woman's Worth, (New York: Random House, 1993), p. 68.

4   ...the cards are already stacked against her, for women are structurally deprived of equal opportunities to develop their capacities, resources and competence in competition with males. ....What is surprising is that little girls don't get the message that they are supposed to be stupid until high school, and what is even more remarkable is that some women resist this message even after high school, college, and graduate school. Ibid., Gillespie, pp. 448-449.

5   Ibid., Gillespie, p. 445.

6   Ibid., Gillespie, p. 453.

7   Op. cit., Gillespie, p. 445 .

8   Op. cit., Jordan, et. al., p. 191.

Chapter Two

A Journey with Jesus!

An effort to understand the intended relationship between female and male proclaimers of the Gospel in today's Church.

Leta: "...you will come to know the truth, and the truth will set you free" (John 8:32). Ah! How we struggle against being free, both as oppressor and as oppressed. To know the truth means that we must struggle to maintain our own freedom, but we must, also, struggle to free those who are still in chains. The sad fact is that there are those at both ends of the spectrum who do not want to be free. To be set free is to challenge tradition, and tradition is extremely comfortable for many, as I mentioned in my story.

The truth is that God created a beautiful and talented being when God created "woman" to whom God gave the blessing of a place within her to co-create with God. No greater blessing is within the grasp of humankind, although the possibilities of co-creation have been limited, for the most part, to that of physically giving birth to another human being. Even the physical aspect of woman's creative power is often controlled by men. A good example is the Roman Catholic Church's stance on abortion. On August 31, 1994, at 7:50 a.m. PBS, Dallas, presented a discussion of the Roman Catholic Church's present stand on birth control and abortion. It was pointed out that their doctrinal position is formulated by men who are not currently living in families, who have never had a female boss, who have never had to negotiate a relationship with a woman and who never have been responsible for putting bread on the table. Accepting the gift of co-creation deals with the responsibility of loving and physically caring for another individual life and the possibilities that forced or unwanted pregnancies limit one's desire or ability to love and nurture such a life. To accept without question the decision as to whether or not to give birth made by those who themselves will never be faced with such a dilemma because of physical and emotional limitations is to deny the wholeness of the gift of God. To accept without question any theological or life-impacting decision made by those who exclude over half of the human creation is to deny the wholeness of God's creation.

Leta & Tom: The other aspects of woman's creative power: thinking, planning, instituting, emoting have also been denied or directed by men. Who decides what Scripture says? Who determines how it is lived-out in the Church and in society?

The Church has modeled a male God and Savior in a hierarchical relationship to God's people. We are suggesting with Rosemary Radford Ruether that Jesus does not model this. Rather, *Jesus revises God-language by using the familiar **Abba** for God. He speaks of the Messiah as servant rather than king to visualize new relations between the divine and the human. Relation to God no longer becomes a model for dominant-subordinate relations between social groups, leaders, and the led. Rather, relation to God means we are to call no man "Father, Teacher or Master" (Matt. 23:1-12). Relation to God liberates us from hierarchical relations and makes us all brothers-sisters of each other. Those who would be leaders must become servants of all.* [10]

Tom: As I affirm this statement I want to question our use of language in reference to God. Can anyone visualize God as anything but male if we continue to use male-centered language?

Leta: Is it language or relationships that are important to this issue? God is much more than either Father or Creator to me, but how I relate to God and perceive how God relates to me is of ultimate importance.

Leta: My first real venture into this freedom movement of women in the Church was called something about "defining our role as Jesus-people." The women for whom I served as Study Leader had only a vague idea about the journey they were taking with me, and my plan was rather nebulous in my mind although rather clearly defined on paper. As the week progressed and some of the women got excited about affirming their role in the Church as Jesus the Christ had intended for them, others began to shake their heads and say, "If anyone but Leta were teaching this, I would not listen." But, Leta **was** teaching it, and they were learning all sorts of new things about Scripture, both Hebrew Scripture and Greek Scripture, as it told **their** story. It all seemed to be a matter of who read the story and where the exclamation points were placed with the voice and with the eyes and with the smile and with the hands. Mainly, with the smile! The smile took away some of their fear. It was a matter of how it was communicated and by whom it was communicated that gave it acceptability. And, the reason Leta could get away with imparting this new information which had always been there in Scripture was because Leta was a returned missionary. The word "missionary" communicates a very special message itself. It is associated with suffering but it is, also, adventurous, for in our United Methodist Church it was the women who raised the money to send the first missionary, a female doctor, to India. Later, when the male ministers demanded the right to manage the money that the women had raised to support that missionary, the women defied them and said, "If we can raise the money, we can manage it." They sent the missionary out because they heard of the suffering of women in India who could not be treated by a male doctor, and they knew that Christ would have been there suffering with them. Thus, a missionary in the Church is part-saint--one who goes and suffers with them--one in whom we can see the Christ at work. The Church has always bestowed a special blessing upon its saints.

Tom: Leta, there is something else that gets bestowed on the Church's saints. They, also, become martyrs. Isn't this a part of what we see in the women's movement toward justice? Becoming aware of the pain and suffering that is being inflicted on the women clergy who speak out against injustice, brought me face to face with the fact of where Christ would be in our Church. With whom would he be standing?

Leta: You are right, and that leads me to the second reason why the people accepted the message that I taught as their own. They knew that the words that I spoke were words gleaned from battle scars. I had struggled to rediscover my own biblical story and my own liberation from the patriarchal interpretation of Scripture given through listening all my life to preaching delivered by male ministers. The knowledge which I imparted to them and its personal affirmation represented my own painful journey into a "foreign country," or as you would say, Tom, into a strange land, just as I had gone to Europe and Africa as a missionary teacher. I was again in that role, and they respected it and me. It authenticated the message which I now tried to communicate to them with the hope of their conversion so that they, too, might journey into this "foreign country" and know the joy of being set free. "Joy" is not used here as a unique or final feeling, for the liberating journey is fraught with much pain. Lynn N. Rhodes says it well, *In joining with women of faith and courage, our hope is to become Christian communities that will be signs that all can nourish and feed each other: communion; that all have a necessary and unique word to give: proclamation; that all have a vocation to fulfill: empowerment.*

*As we work for communities of friendship and solidarity we embody
the hope that we can dare to care passionately for each other, be
vulnerable, and forgive each other. We live out, in different contexts
and in fragments of time, expressions of the vision of relationships of
loving mutuality and justice.* [11]

The ah-ha moments for me seemed to come at very special times,
times when I was not necessarily working on something which had to
do with my new-found interest in the feminist movement but rather
when I would be preparing a sermon or a Sunday School lesson, times
when a Scripture which I had read many, many times before took on
new meaning probably because I could never go back to reading
anything as I had in the past after having been liberated from old ways
of thinking about women in the present-day Church. The book that
opened our eyes in that study group was, **_We Belong Together +
Churches in Solidarity with Women_** by Sarah Cunningham and its
companion guide by Barbara A. Horner-Ibler. It was there that my
thoughts of God, my theology, began to reach out, even to explode, as
I realized that, *Women have been a part of the church's story from the
beginning. Mary, the mother of Jesus, said yes to God's gift of a child
(Luke 1:38). Martha, sister of Lazarus, was among the first to
announce her belief in Jesus as Messiah (John 11:27). Women were
there at his crucifixion (see Matthew 27:55 ff.); Jesus appeared first
after his resurrection to Mary Magdalene (Mark 16:9). "Certain
women," including Jesus' mother, were with the disciples in the upper
room "devoting themselves to prayer" following Jesus' ascension and
preceding Pentecost (Acts 1:12ff).*

*Why have we been so blind to the New Testament evidence that
women too were disciples of Jesus, were founders of churches in their
houses (Acts 16:11-14, 40), were deacons (l Timothy 3:8ff.) and
teachers and preachers (Acts 18:26)? The evidence is all there if we
read the New Testament carefully. ...*

*Despite the probable suppression of evidence of women's presence
in the early church, there is enough evidence remaining in the
historical record to make it quite clear that Jesus was proclaiming a
new understanding of relationships between men and women. As one
of the earliest confessions of the church proclaims: there is no longer
Jew or Greek, slave or free, male and female, but all are one in Jesus
Christ (Gal. 3:28).* [12]

The Greek Scripture begins with the acknowledgment and
affirmation of the role of women in the proclamation of the Good
News as Matthew gives the first and only genealogical chart in the
Holy Scripture which lists five women. Might it be that a patriarchal
church chose to cover up the story that women were deeply involved in
the birthing and the nurturing, the whole process of bringing God's

plan to fruition.

Bringing this closer to home, my own life experience of growing up in a family where my mother was the disciple and my father did not attend church was an early awareness of how important following Jesus was to women. My challenge of this reality and of my father's power in the family in relation to the church impacted my life.

Tom: Before we move on, I would like to speak to that ah-ha moment of yours that came through reading. As you know, I come from the television age and am very visual. Just as your ah-ha moment came when your were not even working on the feminist movement, my ah-ha moments come when I least expect them. I can never look at prime time television without constantly being struck by the demeaning roles in which women are placed. All of our culture seems to contribute to continuing the subordination of women. I keep asking myself how I can relate the Scripture of the preaching moment to what I witness during the week.

Leta: That's great, Tom, because I keep asking, "How will it preach?"

I want to move now to what for me is the most significant event to underscore the importance of women to the proclamation (communication) of the Gospel. Proclamation, who has the right to proclaim and how the message is proclaimed is the heart of this paper. With my "new glasses" I pick up Mark 16:9-11 (Longer ending) and Luke 24:1-12, the biblical accounts of resurrection morning: *Now after he rose early on the first day of the week, he appeared first to Mary Magdalene, from whom he had cast out seven demons. She went out and told those who had been with him, while they were mourning and weeping. But when they heard that he was alive and had been seen by her, they would not believe it.*

In this reading it is clear that Mary was the very first missionary after the resurrection. She went out and told the Good News of the resurrection. She told it first to those who should have already known it. For the first time I began to ask why the male disciples whom we have revered for 2000 years as courageous and faithful tellers of the Good News were not at the tomb themselves to see and to hear the story first-hand. Why had I never heard a sermon about the courage of the women who went to the tomb? Mary Magdalene never slowed down, according to this version, when she was told to go and tell the Good News. It never crossed her mind, according to the Markan Scripture, to doubt, but the male disciples who should have believed if anyone should have, did not believe her. They had to go verify it themselves. Why? Because they did not believe what Jesus had told them about his resurrection or because a woman was the first to hear and to tell the Good News? How could Jesus have been so wrong in his understanding of the patriarchal structure? Or, was he wrong? Were his male disciples among those who would hear but never believe? Why was a woman, trusted by Jesus, the first to see and to believe that Jesus was the resurrected one? We hear the story of Peter's great faith. We often hear sermons on how Thomas doubted but not on the text, "...and they did not believe it," meaning the male disciples. What is the real message hidden herein, who decided to hide it and why?

Tom: I would like to key into your question about who were the oppressed? Ruether says, *It is the women of the oppressed and marginalized groups who are often pictured as the representatives of the lowly. The dialogue at the well takes place with a Samaritan woman. A Syro-Phoenician woman is the prophetic seeker who forces Jesus to concede redemption of the Gentiles. Among the poor it is the widows who are the most destitute. Among the ritually unclean, it is the woman with the flow of blood who extorts healing for herself contrary to the law. Among the morally outcast, it is the prostitutes who are the furthest from righteousness. The role played by women of marginalized groups is an intrinsic part of the iconoclastic, messianic vision. It means that the women are the oppressed of the oppressed. They are the bottom of the present social hierarchy and hence are seen, in a special way, as the last who will be first in the Kingdom of God."* [13]

Has the situation changed any in the present day? Who are the marginalized, oppressed, outcast of today's society? It appears to us that women are still treated with very little regard even in the Church. There are still very few churches who have women in pastoral leadership. There are women who are pastors of small churches and associate pastors in large congregations, but the real power positions within the Church are still controlled by the male dominated hierarchy. Interestingly enough, when an accounting is done on church attendance, we find that the majority of those who attend worship services are women. Could this be because they are oppressed, and, because of their status as marginalized, they can actually hear what the Word has to say?

Leta: As a pastor of a congregation filled with widows and being a widow myself, I understand in a much more significant way why God was adamant with God's people that widows be cared for and how Jesus spoke of the gift of the widow as "all she had." Perhaps it is that out of their pain of loneliness and their neglect by the Church, they are open to any message of love.

I would like to continue the discussion of the Scripture I mentioned above concerning the resurrection. It is the Gospel of Luke 24:11-12. "But these words seemed to them an idle tale, and they did not believe them. But Peter got up and ran to the tomb; ...amazed at what had happened." How could the story of the resurrection which Jesus himself had foretold be considered "an idle tale" except that it was told by women, and women could not be taken seriously in that day and age despite all that Jesus had done to affirm women. Has it changed much in this day and age? Are we still listening with plugged-up ears for Jesus to speak? Mary and the women did not "marvel." They "believed," and they went forth to tell the Good News. Peter "marveled," because evidently he had not "believed" that what Jesus told him before he died would ever take place.

Tom: First of all, we need to remember that this story was recorded by men. Women are known for the tales they carry. Remember, when we want to cast aspersions on a belief, we mark it by calling it "an old wife's tale," never an old husband's tale. Men never carry idle tales. Leta, you said that the women believed and Peter marveled. We know that marveling is not the same as believing. Marveling always leaves an element of doubt. When the pharisees endeavored to trap Jesus by asking him the question of whether it was lawful to pay taxes to Caesar, they marveled at his response. This did not mean that they suddenly began to believe in him as the messiah; rather, they simply were struck by the genius of his answer.

Leta: As I considered this ah-ha moment of discovering that these women who were first at the tomb were also the first missionaries. I remembered with laughter, with "that smile," how, as a missionary, I had always identified with Paul, never with Mary and the women, for before this moment, I had never heard or paid attention to the story of their mission moment. I was not supposed to hear that message. It would have disturbed the status quo. It would have caused me to question how "...the New Testament canon "is a product of the patristic church, that is, a theological document of the 'historic winners'", [14] and women were not the winners. I wonder how many times in the past women have read that story and celebrated the fact that women were the first to believe the resurrection story and to spread the Good News. If a woman had been included in the writing and the remembering of the Story as it became Scripture in the early Church, would we still be facing the problems of effective witnessing being limited by power?

Tom: It seems to me that if women had been the ones entrusted with the sacred task of transmitting the story of the faith, somehow their intent would have been to include the men as equal partners in the task, not to mention the power that the task confers.

Leta: Even before the rereading of the resurrection event, I thought to myself, "There was the Samaritan woman at the well, the one who obviously had not been cared for properly by her people as God required or she would not have had to seek out several men for protection, the one Jesus went out of his way and stepped out of custom to affirm, the one who was a missionary long before the male apostles cut their apron strings from Jesus (John 4:3-30, 39-42). She went back to her village to proclaim the Good News of a savior, a liberator, one who, by his choosing to go against custom in order to witness to God's love for her, said to her that all that society had pushed upon her was wrong, that she no longer had to bear the burden of the men who had used her." "Listen," she said to others, "there is one who can make even me feel whole and happy. Celebrate this Good News with me." Now that took courage. That took chutzpah. And, to think, Jesus initiated it all. Not the woman, but Jesus. Verse 27 tells us that Jesus' disciples came and "marveled" that he talked with a woman and continues with saying that they did not question him as to why he was breaking with religious tradition. Why, I wonder, did they not ask him. I wonder why they marveled. They had observed his behavior and his attitude of inclusion of women as they traveled with him. This was not a new thing. I wonder as well why she has not been celebrated as a missionary, as one so full of the Good News that she could not contain herself. That is liberation. That is resurrection as well.

Tom: This is a perfect example of how Jesus' maleness did not get in the way of his being her liberator/savior. She did not even have to ask Jesus for the living water. Jesus gave to her the wholeness that she needed.

Leta: Rita Nakashima Brock tells us that, *Jesus as liberator calls for a renunciation, a dissolution, of the web of status relationships by which societies have defined privilege and deprivation. He protests against the identification of this system with the favor or disfavor of God. His ability to speak as liberator does not reside in his maleness but in the fact that he has renounced this system of domination and seeks to embody in his person the new humanity of service and mutual empowerment. He speaks to and is responded to by low-caste women because they represent the bottom of this status network and have the least stake in its perpetuation. ... Jesus is the one who morally* *transcends patriarchy. Hence Jesus is the authority and evidence of female Christianity.* [15]

Leta: My thoughts move on to the time when Jesus stopped by Bethany (Luke 10:38-42) to visit with Mary and Martha and Lazarus, his friends. *Now as they went on their way, he entered a certain village, where a woman named Martha welcomed him into her home. She had a sister named Mary, who sat at the Lord's feet and listened to what he was saying. But Martha was distracted by her many tasks; so she came to him and asked, "Lord, do you not care that my sister has left me to do all the work by myself? Tell her then to help me." But the Lord answered her, "Martha, Martha, you are worried and distracted by many things; there is need of only one thing. Mary has chosen the better part, <u>which will not be taken away from her.</u>*

I tried to recreate in my mind the scene that is described where all the men must surely have been dialoguing about religious matters with Jesus the rabbi, the teacher, or perhaps they were recounting some of the "revival stories" in which many of them had taken part. And there was Mary, plopped right there in the midst of the group where everyone, including Mary, must have known that only men should be. What did a woman know about theology or revivals? Yet, Mary did know from her experience with Jesus that around Jesus women had a special value as illustrated in his acceptance of the nameless woman at Simon's house, in his seeking out the Samaritan woman at the well and in his story of the widow and the woman caught in adultery. I could imagine them telling about the feeding of the 5,000 men (not counting the women and children, of course) and Mary's saying, "Don't you know that little boy's mother was so proud of her son and of his remembering what she had taught him about sharing with one's neighbor!" Jesus would have liked that, I'm sure. But, here is Martha, doing what women have always faithfully done--putting off the fun in order to be the perfect hostess. How many programs have I sat through where women always ended up by saying, "Thank God we aren't all like Mary! The real work would never get done if we were." The real work. By insisting that the real work is cooking and pouring and cleaning, we as women have denied our own desires to be a part of the action which, is, of course, what the men are doing. What the men are doing is power-filled: the decision making, the writing and the telling of The Story. By defining cooking and pouring and cleaning as the real work, we assured that we were left out of The Story. And, Jesus says, "Oh, Martha, think about what is important and join Mary here beside us." Yes, it is written a bit differently, but, knowing the bits that slip in now and then about Jesus, I'm sure that he not only affirmed Mary but invited Martha in and that he taught a lesson to all the others. That lesson was: Women have valid thoughts and words to communicate to us. They are more than kitchen maids. They were created by a loving God to co-create with God. What did that communicate to the men? Why did generations later both the women and the men act out a different way of communicating where men discussed and women went back to the kitchen with Martha and forgot the joy of discussion and men forgot what Jesus said and demanded that women serve under them rather than take part in ministry with them? Does power have anything to say to this? What about the Gospel that portrays a Jesus relating to women in the same manner in which he related to men, talking with them in the expectation that they understood his message of mutual love and concern for all peoples.

Another remarkable part of this Scripture is when Jesus says that Mary has chosen the better part, "...which will not be taken from her." That is powerful! Who decided to take it away? When was it taken? We do know that by the time that the organization of the early Church began to take definite form, IT was taken away, for Mary could no longer sit with the church leaders and share equally in the listening and the teaching.

In my own experience I am reminded of a dinner where three United Methodist churches came together. Two of the churches were pastored by male clergy persons. In jest one of them said, "Leta, since your church is pastored by a woman your people must stay and wash the dishes." This brought about a tremendous upsurge of support for me by my parishioners and it said to me, "this is no longer a laughing matter. Mary has come out of the kitchen, and does not want to return."

Tom: I've got two thoughts that come to mind. First, I would like to continue your idea of what was taken away. It seems to me that not only are the Marys deprived of the opportunity to sit and discuss the issues at hand, but what about the Peters and the Matthews who are deprived of the very special insight that women bring to any encounter? The second idea that I want to respond to, Leta, is that you said that the women miss out on the real work--the stuff that is "power-filled," as you say. It seems to me that Jesus gave us the example that we are to be servants of others. Why, even the stoles we wear as ordained clergy are reminders of the towel that Jesus used to wash the feet of his disciples. Isn't the work that we are called to do--the pouring, the cleaning, the cooking--the menial tasks, are not these the tasks that remind us of who we represent?

Now, I know that there is a very valid argument that can be made concerning my preceding statements. It could be pointed out that it is this line of argument that was used by the slave owners during an earlier period in the history of the United States to validate the lot of the slave. The slave owners would tell the slaves that the Bible teaches that slaves were to obey their masters. I can even imagine that slaves were told that this was the Christian thing to do.

I realize that saying that the menial work that women are relegated to is the real work only serves to perpetuate the status quo. I am not suggesting this argument be used for that purpose. What I am suggesting is that maybe, just maybe, women can take on the task of teaching men in the Church what it truly means to be a servant. I believe that something is valuable only when people give it value. I think that was a part of what Jesus tried to teach us--that our value system is all wrong. We place value in achieving positions of power only when those positions mean something to others. If everyone holds the same power, then it is no longer something to be hoarded or envied. Rather, if that scenario were played out, then power would only be something that was shared and utilized for the good of all.

Leta: First of all, Tom, women have been doing those menial tasks from the beginning of time and calling them the real work. My evaluation is that women have received no real affirmation for these tasks, and if what you say is correct, then men are slow learners and we better find another way to celebrate the message of servanthood which Jesus modeled. One of my female colleagues remarked after having served under five senior pastors, "I am worn out with teaching them. Will I always have to start from scratch." Because of our having silently accepted those tasks as our work, we have been kept away from the power and status that does make a difference in our world.

This concept of power is tied to money. The male pastors are given status and power by paying them large salaries. The tasks which you describe as "servanthood tasks" have no monetary value and thus no power in our society. Could servanthood be the loving action of empowering others to experience full servanthood rather than being defined as washing dishes and feet? Yet, we can never forget that Jesus did wash feet.

I move to the magnificent story in Mark 14:3-9: *While he was at Bethany in the house of Simon the leper, as he sat at the table, a woman came with an alabaster jar of very costly   ointment of nard, and she broke open the jar and poured the ointment on his head. But some were there who said to one another in anger, "Why was the ointment wasted in this way? For this ointment could have been sold for more than three hundred denarii, "and the money given to the poor."*

trouble her? She has performed a good service for me. For you always have the poor with you, and you can show kindness to them whenever you wish; but you will not always have me. She has done what she could; she has anointed my body beforehand for its burial. Truly I tell you, wherever the good news is proclaimed in the whole world, what she has done will be told in remembrance of her.

A nameless woman entered a place where women had no place except as kitchen maids. She communicated with her very presence a message that was not soon forgotten. Courage? Commitment? A bit of both. The men were offended. Who let a woman in on the power lunch? Didn't she know that high powered decisions were made in places like this while the bread was being broken or in men's rooms where the body was being relieved? [16] "What possessed her?" they all asked. And, Jesus spoke up and said in words similar to these, "She is the only one present who has any understanding of what is about to take place. You call yourselves my disciples and yet you do not respect me or honor me. Even though your name, Simon, will be remembered and hers forgotten, her act of love will be recounted time and time again 'in memory of her.'" Don't you just love it? I do. Here is Jesus saying over and over again that women know what the Gospel, the Good News, is all about, but twenty centuries later men are saying, "Let us tell you women how to proclaim the Good News." The sad news is that women, too, who make up the majority of our congregations often reject "the nameless woman" story and place women back out on the street, away from the power lunch. Diane Tennis speaks to exactly this issue in her article, ***The Loss of the Father God: Why Women Rage and Grieve,*** " Women also suffer in the wake of the exposure of needy men, which is why women collaborate in keeping the myth alive. It is like facing the emperor without any clothes. If we all pretend he is dressed, he might just as well be." [17] Are we frightened at assuming the responsibility for proclaiming the Good News? And, then, let it be said, that despite Jesus' word that the telling of The Story will include her, "Even her name is lost to us. Wherever the gospel is proclaimed and the Eucharist celebrated, another story is told: the story of the apostle who betrayed Jesus. The name of the betrayer is remembered but the name of the faithful disciple is forgotten because she was a woman." [18]

A story from the Greek Scriptures points out poignantly how women were isolated from the community simply by virtue of being a woman. In Mark 5:21-34 the story is told of a woman whose period had lasted for twelve years. During that full twelve years, by virtue of her flow of blood, she had been considered unclean and placed outside the community. She did the unthinkable. She came up from behind him, obviously touching some of the men in the crowd surrounding Jesus--also, taboo--and simply touched his robe. Somehow, she sensed that this Jesus really did love as humankind is supposed to love. Instead of rebuking her, as I am sure all the crowd expected him to do, he turned to her and said, "My daughter, your faith has cured you. Go in peace, free forever from this trouble." *Free forever from this trouble.* Was it only the flow of blood from which she was freed? Or, was the isolation from and subordination to the male-led community her gift of liberation?

In using the word "frightened," I must move to discussing why this could be an appropriate feeling for women in the Church. This takes me back to the Hebrew Scripture and what it says about the place of women. A cursory glance brings forth an avalanche of frightening history of male use of power over women. Rhodes reminds us that,

A major issue for such women is therefore to be clear about who has power and who needs empowerment. "It is not that power itself is evil," says one. What is evil is "power over, not shared power. It's pretty painful not to have power. Look at the faces of battered women, the poor, refugees, minorities--there is pain because of their lack of power. It is shared power I seek." This understanding of power--rejecting dominating power and affirming shared power--is essential for analyzing the meaning of any established authority. [19]

One must remember that Jesus grew up learning by heart the stories of the God of Wrath of the Hebrew Scripture and of male power over women. To deny this fact is to lose the opportunity to explore where in his upbringing he was introduced to one who taught him how to respect all persons and how to nurture and care for them. Could that have been his mother Mary or even his father Joseph who respected God enough to step out of custom and take a pregnant Mary for his wife? Brock tells us, "If Jesus is reported to have been capable of profound love and concern for others, he was first loved and respected by the concrete persons of his life." [20]

Jesus was an exciting storyteller. To emphasize the importance of the stories that Jesus learned, I quote from Phyllis Trible *Stories are the style and substance of life. They fashion and fill existence. From primeval to eschatological vistas, from youthful dreams to seasoned experiences, from resounding disclosures to whispered intimacies, the narrative mode of speech prevails. Myth, parable, folk tale, epic, romance, novella, history, confession, biography--these and other genres proclaim the presence and power of the story.* [21]

So, "the style and substance of life" for Jesus and for all of us today who are familiar with the Hebrew stories is found therein.

Tom: I grew up with the stories of faith about Jesus which greatly influenced my life and only now realize how important the stories he grew up with were to him. There is a wealth of experience in these stories that maybe can enlighten us concerning the roles of women and men and how each were valued, or devalued. Although the stories were written by men, I believe if we read between the lines, we may be able to discern how the message that women are to be subordinate to men has been systematically passed on from generation to generation.

In the very beginning of the biblical story (Genesis 3) we come upon a possible start of the problems we have inherited today. Eve is portrayed as the one who got Adam into trouble. Ever since then, women have had to live with the bad rap that they caused the whole dilemma of sin. No one ever thinks to place any blame on Adam. At least Eve had the temerity to consider what the serpent was saying. Adam just sort of goes along with the program and does what Eve tells him to do. Doesn't Adam have a brain, did he not see the tree that God pointed out to him? Could he not distinguish that the fruit came from the forbidden tree? If Adam had what it took to be the leader, the power broker, in this idyllic place, why could he not decide on his own to eat or not to eat? Now, I'm not excusing Eve at all for having disobeyed God's instructions. All I am saying is that Adam didn't prove trustworthy in the leadership role. Why is it then that he continued to be the leader?

Leta: I often wonder about the biblical interpretation of the story of Adam and Eve. Did Eve abdicate her power? Who decided to write the story about God giving her the subjugated role? Was it written while she was in the kitchen doing the real work, being the servant, making sure that Adam was taken care of? It appears that this is where it all began with Eve having the responsibility of supporting and making sure that Adam was a success. Men have chosen to perpetuate that story because it is to their benefit to make God responsible. Why have we as women wanted to perpetuate it? What do we gain?

Tom: I don't know that women gain anything from perpetuating the Adam and Eve story where the women are given the subservient role. I wonder if a large part of the reason might lie in the overt psycho-social development that women go through from birth, where what is learned is that women have a place that is subservient to men and as long as they stay in their place they will be "taken care of?" What about the story (Genesis 16: 1-16 21: 9-21) of Abraham and Sarah? Here we have a woman being treated as an object rather than a person of equal value. Abraham, seeking to keep his own hide out of hot water, persuades his wife to tell people that they are brother and sister, not husband and wife. Even though Abraham knows that by telling people this, he is placing Sarah in jeopardy of being taken against her will by powerful men in foreign places. Yet, we hold up Abraham as the Father of the faith. We accord great and high honor to Abraham, while Sarah is only known to us because she is his wife. Though Sarah gave birth to Isaac, it was Abraham that would be known as the Father of all nations. This is an example of how women are used and abused for the sake of men, because they are denied the power to make decisions that directly affect their very lives or to tell the story.

Who can forget the story of Tamar, the daughter-in-law of the King of Judah (Genesis 38: 1-30). Judah didn't play it straight with Tamar; however, Tamar through her wisdom, received what was due her. But, the point being, other than through trickery and deceit, Tamar had no recourse to stand against the King of Judah. What the King said was final. Tamar was only a woman and as such had no rights or allies to speak in her defense. In the end Tamar proves to be the wise and righteous one in the story, but she was still powerless and alienated. Even so, the King of Judah said, "She is more righteous than I." Even more powerful to me as I present the case of Tamar is that I never knew that story until I began to prepare for this project.

Leta: As these stories are told, I am reminded again of how women have had to use the bodies that God created in such beauty to gain recognition from men when, in effect, their intellect was most often considered of little value to them. Tamar, the daughter-in-law of the King of Judah, was the only one among these stories where her intellect enabled her to win what was rightfully hers. It would appear in the act of creation God intended a mutuality which was rarely affirmed in the Hebrew Scriptures.

Tom: Leta, how about the other Tamar who was the virgin daughter of King David, princess of Judah (2 Samuel 13: 1-22). She is violently raped and humiliated by the King's eldest son with her father's passive permission. Once all that is done to her, she is discarded like trash. Even though Absalom, her full brother, was responsible for her and knew the wrong done to her, he chides her not to take the incident to heart. How ridiculous! Tamar has just been used and abused and she is not to take it to heart! Tamar is left alone with no hope of a real life after this violent incident. The last we hear of her is when she is relegated to dwelling in the house of her brother, Absalom. The way the story is told, Tamar only serves as a backdrop for the real story which is about Absalom. Again we have the women being treated unjustly and no one seems to get too excited about it. Oh sure, Absalom eventually kills Amnon for his despicable deed, but why?

Was he vindicating his sister, Tamar, or was he vindicating his own pride because some-thing that belonged to him had been abused by someone else?

There is yet another story about the rape, murder, torture, and dismemberment of an unnamed woman which is almost too horrible to remember (Judges 19:1-30). A traveling man and his wife/concubine stopped for the night in the house of an old man. The host, in order to protect his male visitor from being raped, tortured, and murdered, gives the visitor's concubine to a group of marauding vandals. After the incident, the man goes out of the place where he is staying and merely says to the woman, "Get up, let us be going." When she doesn't get up, he threw her on his donkey, takes her home and cuts her up and sends out the pieces of her mutilated body to the twelve tribes of Israel. The tribes of Israel get incensed over what has happened to this poor man. ***WHAT ABOUT THE WOMAN?*** No one seems to care about the woman and the evil and violence that has been done to her. Isn't this another story which approves of men using and abusing women for their own disgusting reasons? This, too, is a new story to me. Do we dare to preach it?

Leta: I can't think of a more awe-some paradigm to illustrate how little value women had as persons at the time Jesus lived. To think of this woman, as the Scripture says, being abused all night long and crawling back to the only protection she knew and reaching out her hand for her last request for some kind of affirmation of her value to someone, is almost overpowering. Surely, God's Spirit witnesses between the lines in the telling of her story, for the intended story is that Israel was without a King and there was no law in the land. Did Jesus read between the lines?

There are a few other stories that must have bothered Jesus and caused him to think in a different way toward women. He must have known that God, whom he called by the loving term, Abba, could not have treated any part of God's creation in the way that the stories are told in the Hebrew Scriptures. How could any loving father offer his virgin daughter to vandals as the host in the story of the unnamed concubine did? How could any loving father murder his daughter (Judges 11:29-35) just to keep a foolish vow as Jephthah did? As Trible says it so well, "Jephthah is praised;" for keeping a promise to God to sacrifice his daughter; "his daughter is forgotten;" "Like the daughters of Israel, we remember and mourn the daughter of Jephthah the Gileadite. In her death we are all diminished; by our memory she is forever hallowed. Though not a 'survivor,' she becomes an unmistakable symbol for all the courageous daughters of faithless fathers." [22] As we reinterpret the story after all these years whereby you and I see the power of the witness of the daughter rather than the commitment to a vow that ignores the value of human life, so Jesus must have seen it 2000 years ago. Isn't it sad that the institutional church has chosen to side with the story of the oppressor rather than the oppressed?

Tom: Leta, it seems to me that probably the most well known story involving the use and abuse of women is the one about the wife of Uriah, the Hittite. Note, I use the name "the wife of Uriah, the Hittite; whereas, as a child, I knew her as Bathsheba, the temptress of good King David. It was only as I began this study that I realized that Bathsheba had been a woman who had no power and suffered the loss of her husband and her sense of personhood.

Leta: Can you imagine how God must have grieved when God's special king lusted after a married woman who was simply carrying out her ritual of cleansing as required by God's law and brutally used her. The wife of Uriah must also have wondered and cried out, "Help me, O God, for I am only a woman, and I have no power against your king."

These are the recorded stories. There must be many more. In all these stories the men are glorified. The women are treated as important only as background to the story. If women had written the stories, how would they be different? The message is clear. One does not have to confront power in order to be punished. One only has to be female and be in the way of power. No wonder there is fear. These are the stories which Jesus knew by heart. Surely, God was present as Jesus deciphered the real meaning of these stories, and as we struggle for their meaning for our lives today in a Church and in a world which is still acting out of a patriarchal mind set.

As we continue on our journey, we celebrate the fact that Jesus, the Christ, stands beside us. Brock says it so well, *He (Jesus) chose to live for himself and the people he loved by challenging the oppressive powers that destroyed what he loved. His risk is a commitment to solidarity with those crushed by oppressive powers and to the expectation that justice must prevail.* [23]

Footnotes

10   Reuther, Rosemary Radford, Sexism and God-Talk. (Boston: Beacon Press, 1983) p. 136.

11   Rhodes, Lynn N., Co-Creating A Feminist Vision of Ministry. (Philadelphia: The Westminster Press, 1987) p. 126.

12   Cunningham, Sarah, We Belong Together—Churches in Solidarity With Women. (New York: Friendship Press, 1992) pp. 2-3.

13   Op. cit., Ruether, pp. 136-137.

14   Op. cit., Cunningham, p. 3.

15   Brock, Rita Nakishima, Journeys by Heart. (New York: The Crossroads Publishing Company, 1988) p. 64.

16   On my Cambridge college staircase—the nursery of statesmen and spies—plotters gathered, conspiring to make or break alliances. ... would retire to a washroom... and plan to do something unspeakable... .Simon Schama, Review of Diplomacy, by Henry Kissinger, "The Games of Great Men," The New Yorker (May 2,

17   Tennis, Diane, "The Loss of the Father God: Why Women Rage and Grieve," Christianity and Crisis, Vol. 41, No. 10, June 8, 1981. New York, NY, p. 164.

18   Fiorenza, Elisabeth Schüssler, In Memory of Her. (New York: The Crossroads Publishing Company, 1985) p. xiii.

19   Op. cit., Rhodes, p. 29.

20   Op. cit., Brock, p. 66.

21   Trible, Phyllis, Texts of Terror (Literary-Feminist Readings of Biblical Narrative). (Philadelphia: Fortress Press, 1984) p. 1.

22   Ibid., p. 108.

23   Op. Cit., Brock, p. 94.

Chapter Three

But They Won't Talk
with a Woman!

*A journey with female clergy persons as they relate to
their male colleagues and to their congregations.*

In the appointive system of the annual conference in which this
project is being tested, ordained women awaiting appointment are
often met with the statement, "But they won't talk with a woman!"
"They" is the Staff-Parish Relations Committee of a certain local
church in need of a pastor. When such a statement is made, it usually
means the end of any consideration or negotiation between that
particular church and the supervisory powers as far as a female pastor
is concerned. Another church must be found who will "talk with a
woman."

A parable from Brian Wren's book, **What Language Shall I
Borrow?** seems very appropriate here:

*It is said that Christ occasionally walks the earth incognito, to see if
the time has come to end all things. The elders of a large American
congregation got wind of this and were given audience. "Sir," they
began, "we have a problem and need your advice."*

*"Speak on," came the reply. "Some years ago our church took an
important step. After much prayer and thought, we knew that the time
had come to include a woman minister on our staff. We searched
diligently and called a young woman, just out of seminary, as our
associate pastor. She worked very well with our senior pastor, but had
only been with us for six months when he had a heart attack and died.*

*We were deeply distressed, but after a time we appointed a search
committee and eventually called another man, younger, with a good
record of ministry. We asked our associate to stay during the transition
and she worked so well with the new minister that it was obvious she
would continue with us. After five years he moved on to another
congregation, and again we cast about, and eventually called a*

returned missionary, who stayed for nearly eight years. And again, our associate was asked to stay on, and again she worked so well with him that we knew we had done well in calling her. She has become indispensable to us, and when she retires next year, she will have worked successfully with no less than seven senior pastors. So you will understand that we have never regretted our decision."

"Well and good," said the Lord, "but what then is your problem?"

"Our problem is this," said the elders. "In the resurrection, whose associate will she be, since she worked with all seven?" [24]

In this project we are attempting to confront justice issues that relate to the differing styles of communication between female and male clergy. Within that scope we have offered that the problem is one of justice, namely power and money. A good starting point for this discussion might center on the different ways that males and females understand the term **power**, and also how accessibility or inaccessibility to power is viewed by each gender group.

In ***A Male/Female Continuum: Paths to Colleagueship,*** Carol Pierce and Bill Page begin their discussion in the first chapter by talking about "The Man's Journey Away From Dominance." In the introduction the continuum which the authors use is set up in a color scheme. Along the continuum the red color section is the part of the continuum that indicates violence, the blue color section is the part that indicates transition, and the green color section is the part that indicates colleagueship. The authors state "...we are now finding that more and more men enter this continuum near the violent end...".[25] What we understand the violent end to represent is that men are conditioned as they grow up to think in terms of being dominant over women. This ingrained sense of superiority makes it very difficult for men to relate to women with a sense of mutuality and colleagueship.
The man who lives within the red section of the continuum expects women to behave in certain ways. He feels comfortable when women function in limited roles--the helping and supportive ones. When women talk about power, it is hard to hear them. If they act nurturing, it is easier. He is used to colluding with women to either act protective or exploitative, with the woman deferring and accepting her role. [26]

Women are also conditioned from childhood to respond to men from a subordinate role.
Middle class women are socialized as young girls to be helpful and yield. If they are "good" and "nice," they are rewarded with being liked. When things are not right they can easily withdraw and quietly

avoid situations. ...Where a man specializes in paternalism in the red portion, a woman becomes adept at maternalism. Maternalism, as used here, does not symbolize the loving care of mother for child. It refers to a woman's need to control others by being helpful in a way that destroys their individuality. [27]

This kind of scenario makes it very difficult for men and women to relate to one another as equals. Both men and women grow up being conditioned to respond to one another by acting out of roles which each has been taught. Men "learn to enter the continuum accepting themselves as superior and then cover it up as adult men with gentlemanly behavior." [28] And women, too, enter the continuum learning to accept themselves as inferior and learn to act out of that role by adapting manipulative practices to get their needs met. Neither male nor female can respond to one another with a sense of collegiality as long as they act out of roles of dominance and subordinance.

When the issue of power comes into play in a relationship between a male and a female, the playing field is not even. [29] According to Jean Baker Miller there is a general view that power is viewed as the ability to dominate.

There have been many definitions of power, each reflecting the historical tradition out of which it comes; also, various disciplines have devised their own definitions (see, for example, McClelland, 1979). An example given in one dictionary says power is "the faculty of doing or performing anything: force; strength; energy; ability; influence"; and then, follows a long string of words leading to "dominion, authority, a ruler"; then come more words, culminating in "military force." I think the list accurately reflects the idea that most of us automatically have about power. We probably have linked the concept with the ability to augment one's own force, authority, or influence as well as to control and limit others--that is, to exercise dominion or to dominate. [30]

As I see it, for women, power is not seen as the ability to dominate but rather is seen as a tool to help others. I believe the power which women use is the power that enables others to succeed in whatever task or endeavor that they are engaged in. This kind of power seeks to help others to grow and to be whatever and whomever that person can be. This kind of power requires an element of interaction and relationship that is not found in the generally accepted notions of power.

Usually, without openly talking about it, we women have been most comfortable using our powers if we believe we are using them in the service of others. ...For example, in "caretaking" or "nurturing," one major component is acting and interacting to foster the growth of another on many levels--emotionally, psychologically, and intellectually. I believe this is a very powerful thing to do, and women have been doing it all the time, but no one is accustomed to including such effective action within the notions of power. It is certainly not the kind of power we tend to think of; it involves a different content, mode of action, and goal. The one who exerts such power recognizes that she or he cannot possibly have total influence or control but has to find ways to interact with the other person's constantly changing forces or powers. And all must be done with appropriate timing, phasing, and shifting of skills so that one helps to advance the movement of the less powerful person in a positive, stronger direction. [31]

It appears to me, after studying Miller, with the ways of defining power being so different among men and women, it becomes extremely easy for the one who is used to dominating to continue to dominate, and the one who is used to having to be subordinate to continue to be subordinate. When the subordinate female dares to ask for power to be shared, the dominant male will likely react negatively to such a request. To share power would mean to give up the ability to completely dominate, and that would be contrary to what the male has been socialized to understand as his role. So it seems that males continue to guard their power jealously, while females continue to be left powerless and without any sense of justice in the world in which we live.

With power being so unequally distributed between males and females, there hardly appears to be the opportunity for justice to become a reality within the sphere of male/female working relationships. A father once reminded his son of the golden rule maxim; "Those that have the gold, make the rules." In terms of justice it would equate to those who have the power decide who gets treated justly. In the designated annual conference for study the ones who "have the gold" are male clergy and particularly those who pastor large congregations.

When we look at the working relationships between male and female clergy, the playing field is tilted even further in favor of men. Not only do men hold the powerful positions within the hierarchy of the Church, but they also have the centuries of male dominated tradition that biases congregations in favor of men being the leaders and power brokers. When women begin to ask to be admitted to the positions of power, the male leaders can say that the congregations are opposed to women being their leaders. This shifts the blame from the males who are really in power to that all too familiar and anonymous "they".

Another way that male clergy protect their positions of power in the

Church is by hiding behind the protection of separation of Church and State that is a part of our history here in the United States. Even though there may be federal laws that prohibit discrimination against persons on the basis of gender, those laws do not apply to the Church. The Church does not have to ordain women, and the Church certainly does not have to open itself up to being told who must be admitted to the seats of power. There is no active affirmative action committee in the designated annual conference, but tremendous effort is put into the understanding of and protection from sexual harrassment charges. Up to this time, as far as we know, no women clergy have been accused of sexual harrassment.

Male clergy have been socialized to understand that it is their right to be in positions of power and that it is their responsibility to protect the women who are subservient to them. Female clergy have been socialized to accept the role of assistant to the one who is in power, the male clergy. Even though it seems that this understanding is clear, there are times when those pushy women try to upset the apple cart. The apple cart gets upset when women try to affirm the role that was clearly modeled by Jesus, which is that all people are of sacred worth.

It has been our experience that only the smaller churches in the annual conference have had to face the question of receiving a woman as their senior pastor--not always because it is their choice but because of small membership and less income, they can only afford a female clergy person. The larger churches often appreciate their women associate pastors but would never consider them for the top position. Many of the members of the larger churches may have a woman for a supervisor in their secular work, but they say when approached with the possibility of having a female as senior pastor of their local church, that Scripture has clearly defined that God is male, Jesus was male, and Jesus chose male disciples to teach and prepare for ministry according to the recorded story; therefore, "We must carry on the tradition of Scripture." The Church has, also, defined the priesthood or ordained ministry as a profession for males only for most of its existence.

The priesthood is not "just another profession" is a widely held view among Christians. For this reason, many people have no difficulty drawing the line and asserting that, although they are firmly committed to women in work and professions, things are going too far when we start tampering with the sacred. [32]

Emily C. Hewitt and Suzanne R. Hiatt go on to explain that women have been negatively associated with magic (for example, the witch hunts in early America in Salem), and since the sacraments have a mystical or magical part, only males can be allowed to handle them properly. In our own Jewish heritage women were considered unclean during their menstrual periods, and, of course, could not even touch anything sacred or even a male person during that time--which, of course, comes around monthly. Thirdly, tradition is important to all people, and an almost 2,000 year tradition has not only said but has acted out the principle that women are not priests.

Nelle Morton says it a bit differently, "But nostalgically the patriarchal religions evoke the old community in which woman was and is invisible." [33] Men have been taught to tune women out, so part of the task of bringing women into ministry, will be in teaching men in the congregations how to hear women when they preach, even simply acknowledging spiritually that they are present. Morton, also, says that, "Images have to do with the senses. They are rooted in feelings. The stimulation of any sense may trigger the functioning of most unreasonable images that have never been brought to consciousness or have never been put to rest. Once the mind is cleared of accumulated blocks, it is free to embrace new images--positive images in all sorts of fresh new ways." [34] It is our experience in the annual conference in which this project is taking place, that the old images still abound, and many blocks are yet to be removed before women ministers will not have to hear, "But they won't talk with a woman."

There is another important issue which must be addressed. When confronted by God with his sin, Adam replied in his defense, "The woman whom you gave to be with me, she gave me fruit from the tree" (Genesis 3:12). Our society has held the woman responsible for children born to unmarried women. Yet, we trust her to rear our children while blaming her for all that is wrong. In one sense we trust her with our future. In another sense we say that she is to blame for what goes wrong. So, for the most part, the system gives her care of the churches which went wrong and became small so that she can nurture them into death. Where there is still life and the possibility for new growth, we appoint men to run them, making the administrative decisions and preaching the message to follow and give the men a female associate who has the job of nurturing the members so that they can live-out the Word communicated from the pulpit.

To underline the above thought, we quote Nelle Morton,
We have learned that men in control of our church tend to consider it a threat to their virility (and resistance against God-created subservience) when women make any effort to participate in top decision making. Further, these men tend to dismiss such women, usually with politeness, by dragging all sorts of red herrings across the issue. [35]

Some of those "red herrings," according to Morton, are: "Her voice is too rasping," "She just doesn't turn me on," "They are men haters."[36] Our own experience with "red herrings" is, "She's bitchy, and who wants a bitchy preacher!" Or, "She is laid-back. We need a real go-getter who has his future before him and will work his head off to prove himself." "We don't want somebody running the church who will always think of her family first."

An example drawn from the studied annual conference is that of the reappointment of a female associate who had worked with a male senior pastor and a male associate for a long period of time. During the time of their service together, the female was never given a compliment by the other associate. After her departure, church members who were being trained for a ministry by the male associate, reported that he said, "I would like to take credit for what I am about to train you to do, but I must say that I learned what I present to you as "pastoral care" by observing "Eve's" ministry while she was among us. Her creativity is astounding."

"It is thwarted ambition that most plagues bureaucracies, subtly encouraging passive-aggression. No matter how hard a man (sic) works, he (sic) can never accomplish enough or be fully recognized for his (sic) efforts," [37] says Scott Wetzler, because most bureaucracies are run by passive-aggressive males. We contend that the above is true in the sense that an annual conference is a bureaucracy which is dominated by males. Our experience shows that many of those males fit the description of a passive-aggressive behavior which is: "Aggressive behavior manifests in passive ways such as obstructionism, pouting, procrastination, intentional inefficiency, and obstinance."[38] Wetzler continues by saying, "Remember: the passive-aggressive man is driven by fear, so while he may want to walk all over you to feel stronger, paradoxically, he's also afraid that he might cause you real pain." [39] We contend that the pain inflicted due to fear in this bureaucracy is visited upon the male clergy as well as upon the female clergy, but it is much better hidden by males. This takes us back to the fact that since the creation story, the message communicated is that it is all right to blame and walk on women but not on men.

Another issue of concern is the different preaching styles of male and female clergy. Women interweave their own personal stories into their messages of how to live-out their faith; whereas, men more often tell stories of other people and those which illustrate how they are different from others.[40] Parishioners generally react positively to the women's preaching, and this appears to cause pain and injustice to the women if they serve under a male senior pastor. The males appear to be saying, "Love me but don't draw too close." The females appear to be saying, "Love me and draw close because you know that I feel as you feel, and I need your closeness." Deborah Tannen speaks of the fact that "There are many kinds of evidence that women and men are judged differently even if they talk the same way. This tendency makes mischief in discussions of women, men and power. If a linguistic strategy is used by a woman, it is seen as powerless; if it is done by a man, it is seen as powerful."[41] She goes on to tell the story of an interview in a newspaper where a husband-wife team who were both psychologists responded to a question, both at the same time. "The man said, 'Subservience.' The woman said, 'Sensitivity.' Both experts were right, but each was describing the view of a different gender."[42] We believe that being sensitive is a sign of seeking "connection;" as explained by Tannen; whereas, connection is obliterated in a subservient situation. Given a congregation made up of more women than men, how is it then that congregations prefer a male senior pastor to preach?

"To be alive today is to live with pain," says Rita Nakashima Brock. "For some of us, our pain is the daily struggle to survive and to find a safe place to live. Others of us work to lift oppressive barriers that silence us and batter us into submission. ...To live with our pain without some comprehension is to exist in the denial of pain or in the overwhelming, intractable presence of it."[43] M. Scott Peck wrote a book beginning with the words, "Life is difficult."[44] Both of these authors contend that many in our society live daily lives which lead us to despair. In our interaction with many of the female clergy in the chosen annual conference for our study, we find that most have given up the fight to be recognized as gifted, "called" people due to the battering into submission of which Brock speaks. Even if they remain in the system, they accept the submissive role as normal. The battle to see, as Brock says, that "Jesus is the one who morally transcends patriarchy"[45] and that he gives them the authority of affirmation is a hard enough concept for women to grasp much less try to teach it to their male clergy colleagues. The idea of justice for others may be acceptable for women but not for themselves, because demanding justice for themselves would endanger the extremely important need in women to remain or to be connected with others--even their male clergy colleagues.

Our task of confronting justice issues related to the differing styles of communication which affect the working relationships between male and female clergy in an annual conference of the United Methodist Church is based on conversations which take place in two consciousness-raising groups, a brainstorming group made up of male and female clergy and personal interviews with individual clergy persons. The two consciousness raising groups, one all-female and one all-male, met for six sessions and discussed their individual situations in ministry as they relate to clergy persons of the opposite sex using ***Women' Growth In Connection,*** a collection of writings from the Stone Center at Wellesley College in Wellesley, Massachusetts, as their guide.

Our original hope in designing this project was that we could bring about dramatic change in the plight of clergy women in an annual conference of the United Methodist Church whereby female clergy persons would be accepted and affirmed in a more just and loving manner, and that this, in itself, would result in better salaries and that women clergy would have their opinions accepted as valid and worthy. As we have begun to explore and prepare for our groups, we have come to the feeling that we need to keep in mind the Gospel lesson Luke 18:1-8. In this lesson a woman goes again and again to the judge to ask for help. Again and again, she is rejected. The judge finally answers, "because this widow keeps bothering me, I will grant her justice so that she will not wear me out by continually coming." The important thing was that the widow felt so strongly about what she hoped for that she never gave up. She believed that what she did was important. The president of the Czech Republic, Vaclav Havel, said that "hope is not about believing that we can change things; hope is about believing that what we do matters."[46] It is our hope that our journey will be no less affirming and that what we do and where we go matters.

Footnotes

24   Wren, Brian, <u>What Language Shall I Borrow? (God-Talk in Worship: A Male Response to Feminist Theology).</u> (New York: The Crossroad Publishing Company, 1989) pp. 216-217.

25   Pierce, Carol and Page, Bill,<u> A Male/Female Continuum: Paths to Colleagueship.</u> (Laconia, NH: A New Dynamic Publication, 1986) p. 13.

26   Ibid., p. 13.

27   Ibid., p. 21.

28   Ibid., p. 13

29   I could see the positive effects of associations with family members when I asked a man who was very highly placed in his organization why he was particularly interested in making sure that women got a fair shake in his organization. He said it was because he had two daughters. "When I saw them coming up at their jobs," he said, "I realized they weren't playing on a level playing field." Deborah Tannen, Ph.D.,<u> Talking From 9 to 5</u>. (New York: William Morrow and Company, Inc.,1994) , p. 217.

30   <u>Op. Cit.,</u> Jordan, et. al., p. 198.

31   <u>Op. cit.,</u> Jordan, et. al.,p. 199.

32   Hewitt, Emily C. and Hiatt, Suzanne R.,<u> Women Priests: Yes or No?</u> (New York: The Seabury Press, 1973) p. 25.

33   Morton, Nelle, <u>The Journey Is Home</u>. (Boston: Beacon Press, 1985) p. xxiii.

34   <u>Ibid.,</u> p. xxii.

35   <u>Ibid.,</u> p. 5.

36   <u>Ibid.,</u> p. 5.

Footnotes

37   Wetzler, Scott, Ph.D., <u>Living With The Passive Aggressive Man.</u> (New York: Simon & Schuster, 1992) p. 192.

38   Warner, Arnold, M.D., Chairman of sub-committee of the Joint Commission of Public Affairs, eds. <u>A Psychiatric Glossary</u>, Fifth Edition, American Psychiatric Association. Washington D. C.: American Psychiatric Association, 1980) p. 104.

39   <u>Op. cit.,</u> Wetzler, p. 51.

40   Nuechterlain, Ann Marie and Hahn, Celia Allison, <u>The Male-Female Church Staff (Celebrating the Gifts • Confronting the Challenges).</u> (New York: An Alban Institute Publication, 1990) p. 7.

41   Tannen, Deborah, Ph.D., <u>You Just Don't Understand.</u> (New York: Ballentine Books, 1990). pp. 224-224.

42   <u>Ibid.,</u> p. 225.

43   <u>Op. cit.,</u> Brock, p. 1.

44   Peck, M. Scott, M.D., <u>The Road Less Traveled (A New Psychology of Love, Traditional Values and Spiritual Growth).</u> (New York: Simon & Schuster, 1978) p. 15.

45   <u>Op. Cit.,</u> Brock, p. 64.

46   Fortune, Marie M., "What You Do Matters," <u>Response</u>. (Cincinnati, OH.: Women's Division, General Board of Global Ministries, United Methodist Church, September 1994) p. 10.

Chapter Four

Come Let Us Reason Together!

An exploration in preparation for our journey in search of justice.

Leta: Entering the journey in search of justice is painful even though we desire justice with all our heart. But the entrance into this journey toward justice for women was one of the most painful ones of my life.

My realization of the implications of the pain I was to experience on this journey on which I was embarking actually began with my scheduled appearance before a group who would decide whether or not to recommend me for ordained ministry. I entered the room knowing that I was well prepared not only educationally but with a wealth of experience in various forms of ministry on a global scale. The people who were to examine me were all known to me to some degree. Some of them I considered to be my special friends in ministry. I felt no fear. I knew that God had called me to serve as God's person in the church that I loved. Knowing this, I had faith that God would never abandon me nor would the Church which had always surrounded me with love. God had been faithful to me since birth in giving me the strength to witness and be loved in a racist hometown, in giving me a mate to stand beside me in protection and love.

My life was a living witness to God's love and faithfulness. I was the first of 65 grandchildren and great-grandchildren to be graduated from high school, and here I was with three degrees, working on my fourth. My family was poor and yet I worked my way through Southern Methodist University. I had spent 11 years in teaching in Africa in countries always in revolution and 12 years in the extremely stressful position of protective services for children. I had survived the death of my husband and was able not only to live but to celebrate wholeness of life. What was I to fear in a committee appointed to judge my gifts for ministry?

LORETTE WILMOT LIBRARY
NAZARETH COLLEGE

How wrong I was! I never in my life had so identified with Daniel in the lion's den or Meshack, Shadrack and Adednigo in the fiery furnace. In fact, I envied them and would have traded places in a minute. I even considered leaving by the closest exit.

The first words spoken were, "Leta is asking to be made a part of the brotherhood [sic], and I know that there is one of the brotherhood [sic] whom she does not even like." It went downhill from there. Accusations were made about 18 months not being long enough for me to stay at the church where my husband had been serving at the time of his death in order to let the parishioners sufficiently grieve. My thoughts whirled in my head. "Well," I thought, "I never did want to be a part of a 'brotherhood' but rather just one of a community of folks who were working together for the good of the Lord." Having grown up in a family with one sister, I knew that it was impossible to like all the people all the time, but I could try to love them. I would fight to the death to defend one of the family but then fight with them behind closed doors, loving them all the time. I was not only confused but I was scared. The thought raced through my mind, "They can't be doing this to Jack's widow." And then I realized that I had used the wrong metaphor in the beginning. The thought that I now had was grounded even in the Hebrew Scripture where widows had God's special protection, and thus that of God's special community. I thought to myself, "This is not the lion's den or the fiery furnace. Those are male images. This is the rape of Uriah's wife by good King David." Most of the ministers remained silent during this event. I recalled how Nathan had said to King David, "...you have not only despised my command, but you have despised me."(2 Samuel 12: 10) Maybe they were silent as they considered the action of abuse of a woman created by God as an action which would bring sadness to God. I sensed that there was some confusion among the ministers. I was later to learn that this situation was typical of an organization which Schaef and Fassel describe in their work, The Addictive Organization.[47]

I was approved and later spent some time by myself crying, a gift I did not allow myself to receive until I was outside the presence of the group. It was interesting when later I listened to the comments of other women who had undergone similar experiences to mine and how they, too, had felt abandoned. Some had been told privately by members of the group that they had "felt" for them but knew that they were strong enough to handle it on their own or that they had meant to be supportive by way of body language. None of my male colleagues, with much less experience in ministry than I had, reported experiences similar to mine.

This event was my first cognitive step into the journey that has led me to acknowledge the injustice that is so pervasive in our church toward women in ministry. For the next several years I learned how to work within the system to a certain degree. I struggled with disappointment, deep sadness and occasional moments of elation when I felt that I knew that I had "worked the system" in order to obtain my goals to serve in ordained ministry. Later I would worry and fret that perhaps I had placed "working the system" over my sense of integrity, since the characteristics of the system were not ones that I admired.[48] By then I was in the doctoral program working on a proposal for a project, and this experience seemed to dominate my life in ministry. With all the above in mind, I decided to call a brainstorming session of both male and female clergy who had served together in some working capacity to either confirm my own experience or to illustrate that it was a one-of-a-kind event. If my experience was validated, then the journey toward justice for women in ministry needed to be made.

Tom: What a journey! Leta, I remember your relating some of your struggles to enter ordained ministry, but somehow when they are presented in this light, I cannot even begin to imagine what would prompt you to struggle to gain entrance into a system that seemed set upon keeping you out. It could only be your calling from God that would give you the courage to stand against efforts to invalidate all of who you are. At this point, I can only see it as the Holy Spirit working in our lives that caused you to invite me to be a part of that brainstorming session.

As I reflect back upon what happened that day, I believe that a real transformation took place in my life as I participated in your group. The stories of pain, oppression, denigration, and outright injustice overwhelmed me. I think that it was at that point that I had found another group of people who were marginalized and whose struggle for justice was one in which I needed to take part. As I participated, I found myself mentally pulling apart from the group to reflect upon what was taking place. I realized that the interchange between the males and females was the healthiest experience of which I had been a part since entering the journey into ordained ministry. You and I still had another stage to go in the ordination process, and I realized that yours would probably be more painful than mine simply because you are female. [49] You and I are now both ordained elders and in full-connection of an annual conference, and what I feared at that moment in time proved to be valid not only for you but for many of the women who made the journey with us. Because that interchange was such an exciting one, I wondered how I could continue to participate in your project. Now we know how.

Brainstorming Session over lunch April 11, 1994

For reporting purposes only, we will temporarily discontinue our dialogue and will report from the position of observer.

Eighteen people were invited to participate in the Brainstorming Session, 10 of whom had been interviewed by Leta beforehand. Counting Leta, fourteen actually participated. Of those participating, there was an almost equal number of male and female clergy present. Three of those present were lay people who have had long experience serving on church staffs where male and female clergy have been appointed. Some males had supervised female clergy, and all women had served as associates at one time. The ages of the participants ranged from the 30s to retired. Three of the persons who were invited to participate had a conflicting called meeting concerning ordination issues. Two of them, because of their interest in the subject matter, made a special effort to come in for personal interviews on their own initiative, and one who was present wanted to extend his participation by staying for an interview. After everyone had gathered, Leta explained again, as she had in her letter of invitation, (See Appendix #1a.) our reason for being there. At the time that the invitation was extended, Leta had intended to develop a questionnaire for use in interviewing selected clergy. Because Leta found that the stories that some of the women shared in the Brainstorming Session differed considerably from those she had heard in her personal interviews with those same women, Leta decided not to do a questionnaire but rather to hold consciousness-raising groups as a more effective means of bringing about change in the system and in individual lives—an ultimate goal of this Project. Because the women's stories changed in the presence of the men, she wondered if they felt intimidated by them and/or if just being present in a group as opposed to a one-on-one situation could have changed their response. In the event that this was so, the decision to organize consciousness-raising groups which would be made up of all one gender with the possibility of a final joint session seemed to be the better solution.

Before Leta could pose the first question at her brainstorming session, one of the male clergy persons took over and made a statement, the essence of which follows: "In a male/female combination of ministers women have a capacity that men do not—the capacity for dealing with other women on a level that men are unable to enter. In a church where there is a male/female combination, the clergy staff will be much stronger than if there were only two men. Men are too much alike, domineering and chauvinistic, and they are not even aware that they are. To act in non-masculine ways they have to think about it. Women can handle certain things much better than men."

In response to this comment the following issues were raised by the group:

—Two women can, also, have as much trouble working together as a male/female combination, and we should just enjoy the combination of men and women as a complement to each other.

—A male clergy person suggested that there is a disparity in assignments in a multi-staffed church. Sacramental (Baptism and Holy Communion) and near-sacramental (marriages, funerals, prayers) assignments are made to males more often than to females.

—Older congregants seem to be more resistant to women, and it was asked what this has to say about our greying congregations? This provoked considerable disagreement, and some female clergy persons pointed out that they found greater opposition from younger female congregants than from older women. They speculated that this related to the fact that a professional woman was a threat to the self-considered value of full-time homemakers.

—Admission of fears were expressed by a female clergy person when she had heard a rumor that the male senior pastor with whom she served would be replaced by a female, which would place her with a female clergy person and thus diminish or destroy her unique female role which she enjoyed while serving with a male senior pastor. As discussion centered around the meaning of "a female presence," the conversation moved into a discussion of the perceived role of any minister. The group was in consensus that the role carries with it a male connotation, such as where the perceived important community news is disseminated (in the mechanic's shop, not in the beauty shop) and the kind of expected important community duties (such as marking off the football field at the beginning of the season rather than joining the book review club).

At this point Leta chose to introduce some specific questions which her field supervisor had helped her to develop.

Reflection: In reflecting upon how the session began, we note that an older male took charge by making the first statement without being invited to do so, which statement related directly to the issue of men automatically assuming control while in the presence of women;

thereby, leading the discussion until Leta intervened. Although his statement was meant to be supportive of women in ministry, we see it as an illustration of a dominant/subordinate understanding of male/female relationships. The fact that he took the prerogative may reflect his assumption of the dominant role or his eagerness for discussion of the subject. This action indicates to us the male orientation toward task as opposed to the female relational emphasis and, also, suggests his assumption that male conversation is more valid, logical and to the point. [50]

Question: Do the different ways that male and female clergy persons express emotion affect how we are perceived by our congregations and by each other on multi-staffed churches? For example, have the female clergy ever stifled crying, or felt the need to stifle, when in conference with male clergy persons or in other situations of leadership for fear of being thought of as a "weak" female?[51]

A male pastor answered first by saying that intense anger sometimes caused him to cry. He had had women interns who, when they cried, he would ask what the tears meant. He said that they told him that their tears did not always have to do with what they were talking about or anything to do with him. We suggest one possible answer is that they did not feel free to share with him as a male in power over them that their tears were connected to him.[52]

The group appeared to agree that men cry with anger and women cry with pain and that these are appropriate situations for each of them to express these emotions. Someone suggested that crying is a very human emotion and that if women cried, the pain was very intense and they wanted it received appropriately. With the continued feminization of the clergy in the church, men should learn more about how to deal with this expression of pain.

One male pastor remarked that he had cried in front of the congregation at times, and the parishioners had expressed to him that they saw it as a strength of character for him. He added that he thought when women cry in front of the congregation that they are perceived as weak. One female clergy person who had cried while leading a particularly poignant liturgical prayer was told by a female parishioner that she needed to "keep a stiff upper lip" but wanted to hug her anyway.

At this point one woman just interjected that she would not want to take the "power" times away from men. Leta asked if it had to be an either/or situation. She queried as to how the group would negotiate power?

All of the women remarked on how they watch very closely what they say to male pastors and how some even watch what they say to men in general. They don't want to come off looking smarter, because smart means power. A woman can be punished for being powerful. [53]

The women let the men win since it seems to be so important to the men and also because they fear retribution. The women voiced their desire to keep peace.[54]   They tied this to a long range vision of, "Where will I be in ten years?" as opposed to short range objectives. The women said that if they are too pushy, they will not advance up the career ladder of the United Methodist Church. One woman said that she spent much more time on relationships, and she believed that men with whom she worked spent more time on tasks which translates itself into power.

The men related that "sacramental" tasks or tasks which put them before the congregation will be assigned by a senior male pastor to the men on staff unless the women associates exert themselves by saying that they really want the tasks. The men said that the women must let the circumstances be known from the beginning. Let the male pastors know that they are unhappy. A couple of the women said that when they actually did do what was being suggested, they paid the price. The senior pastor would have his secretary call them in from important and/or enjoyable things such as continuing education in order to ask a rather mundane question of them—a show of who has the power, who is in charge.

Justice issues: Leta brought up the issue of justice. A male pastor said, "We male pastors and our congregations will not change until a female is appointed pastor of a large church with a male associate." Leta asked him how it felt to know that fact or even to express it in front of the female pastors present. His response was that it had nothing to do with feeling. It was reality, pure and simple.

Comments: A person experienced in working with groups, upon reviewing the material with Leta noted that the only time that women spoke forcefully, they had changed their story from that given during their interview with her or they kept asking for reassurance from the group that the conversation would not leave the room. Still the words were delivered with what appeared to be fear and trembling. Could this behavior be evidence of the women's need to nurture and not to offend the men present in the room? [55]

Question: Were you ever given a job description and an opportunity to discuss your gifts and grace for ministry? If so, who initiated the discussion?

Only one out of the group had had such a conversation with a senior pastor or a congregational committee. Most were given a job description and told to run with it. The one who had had the opportunity to share what she felt to be her strengths and her weaknesses with her senior male minister felt affirmed in ministry and has continued to feel so. The male clergy persons had not expected to be consulted about their gifts and grace, but they often did get work assignments which they wanted. Because one female associate was very open with her male senior pastor about his criticism of her, he stated that he felt that he had grown more sensitive to her particular problems as a woman in ministry and was more able to recognize her gifts and made adjustments accordingly.

This conversation evolved into the next question concerning differing communication styles between male and female clergy persons.

Question: Are you aware of how the way we say things differently as males and females affects the way we carry out our ministry?

One female associate said that she always approaches the male senior pastor from a "feeling" point of view. She stated that she never sees him approach anyone that way, but she said that she thinks that he understands her when she does this. When she fills in for him in leading staff meetings, she chooses to lead according to the male model which, she says, is short and quick and task-oriented. She further stated that all the staff appreciates getting things over with in a hurry without much discussion and then getting back to work. It was suggested that accepting this model as the norm begs the question as to whether or not the staff meeting, the community gathered, is not also carrying out a very valid form of work. Why is staff meeting not considered "work"?

Another female, in dealing with this question, turned to a male with whom she had served and commented that when he led them through meetings quickly, they got more work done. He responded, "Work or tasks?"

One female found that she wanted advice on her performance more often than the male senior pastor wanted to give it. He told her that if he had to spend time in checking up on her, he did not need her on the staff. She felt assured that this meant that he trusted her. [56]

Another issue spoken to dealt with how a male and female clergy team can sometimes work well together until another male comes on the scene. More than one female clergy person present had been in such a situation. One of them told how she thought it important to take the blame for the confusion and hurt which takes place in such a situation and said that she felt better when she "got her act together."

One woman discovered that when the male senior pastor told her that he would think about something, he really meant, "No," and not to bother him again.

Question: How does money enter into relationships?

A male and a female who had once both been associates on the same larger staff related a story about how raises in salary were handled by the senior pastor who is no longer in their conference. They both understood that he was in charge, and he had told them that salaries were not negotiable. The male clergy person perceived that, despite the spoken word, there was always room for negotiation and spent no time worrying about doing so. He just negotiated. He always got more than was first presented by the senior pastor, as did all the males on the staff, according to him, because they bargained with the senior pastor.[57] The female clergy person always looked at the paper handed her by the senior pastor with her salary written on it and considered any raise in salary a real gift. She would never have dreamed of asking for more, she said, although she finally found out that despite her greater tenure, she received less than her male colleagues.[58]

One clergywoman presented her request for a raise to the church committee charged with that task and was later told by the senior pastor that she did not have the same rights of access to that committee as did he. All agreed that despite the fact that associate pastors are under full-appointment by the bishop, the senior pastor is always in charge. Leta reminded us that we were not discussing associates but the role of women in ministry.

The discussion on money led very easily into a conversation on issues of power. All agreed that money is power. The "Power Place," where money and all other important problems are handled, are places from which women are barred—over lunch, while playing golf and most importantly in the rest rooms. The women clergy present had never been invited to lunch by a male senior pastor and surely never will be with the recent emphasis on sexual harassment, they decided. Even if they play golf, they will never be asked to do so for many of the same reasons that they will never be asked to lunch. The women present had not been aware of the business conducted in the rest rooms, [59] but the men present agreed that that is the place where they all go when anything gets boring. Men pointed out that males ventilate on the golf course. All of the above were accepted as givens by the female clergy. There was nothing they could do to change the situation, but it still leaves them powerless. The group seemed to agree that power relates directly to who has the senior pastor's ear. Leta suggested that we give thought as to how we can handle this use of power in order to find a way to overcome it and work toward better relationships in order to serve our congregations in more loving ways. Equally important is that facing up to the use of power and powerlessness is a way of caring for ourselves. She, also, suggested that we talk about what the discrepancy in pay meant to all of us, both male and female.

The female clergy person who found that all males on the staff, not just clergy persons, were making higher salaries than she dealt with this "grief" by convincing herself that salary is not a judgment of one's worth but rather evidence of one's negotiating skills. She added that knowledge is power but still limits how far one can go.

Out of the blue one woman said, "We (women) are also very competitive." Is this woman inferring that women are not as good as men as negotiators even though they have the same competitive instincts?

Question: What style of communication do you see in staff meetings, male or female?

A male immediately said that since the senior pastor, who, at this point in time, is always male, leads the staff meetings, the male method of communication will predominate or as someone has already suggested, the female when left in charge will adopt the male style "because," as she said, "it gets the job done faster."

First of all, the males said that they felt that they needed to take care of the women present but could not say how they do this. One said that he learned that women can take care of themselves.

Women seem to go for consensus and gathering of opinions; whereas, the males say, "This is what we are going to do." If a woman approaches it this way, she is labeled as pushy and aggressive, according to the men present. If a man does the very same thing, he is considered a great leader, they further stated. Leta suggested that she personally does not consider that a sign of great leadership but rather a way of instilling fear in those who serve under him.

Women found it easier to be absent while attending to family matters, because parishioners expect women to do that. It is accepted that women are more relational than men, they said. Men are not encouraged to be family-oriented. It is thus hard for them to work with staff as a family. [60]

Although staff meetings are required for most present, no one was allowed not to show up without prior approval or to change the meeting time or date but the senior pastor, according to all present. All other staff were expected to fit into his schedule.

It was suggested that the use of power could be attributed to seniority and not to gender. The females all joined in chorus to say, "No, it is gender!"

One female minister said that males could miss staff meetings and even flaunted it by laughing and talking with the senior minister in her presence, knowing that she had been reprimanded by him for missing staff meeting.

It was suggested that there is an advantage to being older—a bit more respect shown even if your were an associate — thus, a bit more power.

Several comments were made about different preaching styles, especially in the use of humor. For some reason or other this was not pursued with any excitement.

The stated closing time arrived, and most of those present had to be back "at work." Some wanted to tarry, but most participants felt there was no more to be said. It is interesting to note that the male who had taken charge in the beginning pointed out that he had to be back at work and that if anything was not covered, it was because everyone had not taken the stated starting time seriously.[61]   The message was delivered in an authoritarian manner—no laughter or smile. He had arrived early. Leta had commented on this fact when she greeted him.

Interviews

While this project was still in the "aborning" stage, several exploratory interviews were conducted by both Tom and Leta with specific questions in mind although they were not posed as such to the person being interviewed. Most of these interviews are not recorded here due to the inability to keep confidentiality and the fear of retribution of those interviewed. This fact in itself is important to note in a study of this kind. The interviews presented below, with the exception of A. B., are composites of conversations which both of us have had with clergy persons of more than one annual conference. We have taken this measure to protect those who have entrusted their stories to us.

A.B.

One of the first interviews was initiated by telephone with the first female clergy person (henceforth, referred to as A. B.) who was ordained an elder in the conference designated for study. The Project was explained, and her conversation flowed freely with almost no encouragement. She felt an urgency to tell her story. A.B. explained that her age and her health might cause some discrepancy in her memory of events, but the conversation is recorded as closely as possible as told.

A.B. was given her local preacher's license in 1937 when she was 17 years of age. During World War II A.B. served as a Chaplain's Assistant. Because she was a woman, she could never bear the title of chaplain although she did the same work as the male chaplains. It was 17 years later, after having been graduated from Perkins School of Theology in 1948, that she was ordained a deacon and placed on probationary membership in an annual conference. She said that she is the first woman ever to receive a Bachelor of Divinity degree from her seminary. Four years later in 1954, A.B. was ordained an elder but remained on probationary status. When the General Conference voted to take women into full-connection, according to A.B., in 1956, she petitioned her annual conference to accept her. They did not. She later contracted cancer and was told that she would have to obtain a statement from a medical doctor stating that she was free of all illness before her case would be considered again, although, continued A.B., the male candidates did not have to meet that same standard. She remembers well an elderly male pastor saying from the floor of an annual conference meeting, "Ah, let's vote the woman in. She's going to die anyway." They did not vote her in, however, until she received the letter of approval from a medical doctor. Nineteen years later, in

1973, A B. was voted into full-connection. By then another woman had already been taken into full-connection.

A.B. can remember clearly how differently she approached ministry and the political system of the church from the manner in which her male clergy colleagues did. The male clergy "were always climbing the ladder, trying to get a bigger church, but I was not interested in that at all. The men found this bizarre." Although she did not retire until the mid-eighties, she said that she found an anti-feminine bias both among her colleagues and among parishioners. She never felt that she was accepted as a full colleague or a pastor in the fullest sense of the word.

C.D.

C. D. was a clergywoman who was not sought out but who openly told her story in an impromptu conversation one day when I explained about my Project to her. She had at one time been very active in what she saw as the "feminist movement" among clergy women in several denominations but particularly among those of her own denomination, United Methodist. Eventually, she had opted out or at least given up the fight. She had grown weary of the struggle to be accepted as an equal to her male colleagues.

As she recalled her years in ministry, she thought that she could see where she had been punished by the male clergy who were in power over her and even by any female clergy who had "climbed the ladder." She even suspected that some of her appointments had been made as punishment—for what she did not know. She surmised that it had to do with her involvement in feminist issues, but she was not sure of this. Her response had been eventually to ignore the connectional system. She had found it hard to push in any way the monetary giving which supports the hierarchical structure which discriminates against women, as she saw it and had personally felt it.

E.F.

E. F. is a male clergy person who wanted to be a part of the Project. His first comment into the interview was, "I see absolutely no difference in the treatment of male and female clergy in our conference." He felt that some of the clergywomen whom he knew just did not feel comfortable in certain aspects of ministry, so he did not worry about it. When he personally had decisions to make which affected his female colleagues, he made certain that they received the same treatment as did his male colleagues over whom he had the same power. He did not worry about anyone's salary but his own, so he did not know if there was any difference between the male and the female clergy.

"Professionally we can never get away from our human sexuality," he said. "It is probably not possible to have a real friendship between male and female clergy colleagues without the sexual element becoming a problem," he stated. When asked how this affects decision-making since men do currently hold the power positions and if he were correct about friendships, women could never really get to know those in power well enough to be considered for the better appointments, he did not see this as a problem. If he were right, there could never be real collegiality between the male senior pastors and their female associates, I suggested. He pondered this question and then replied that he wondered why women would want to be in groups in which they didn't feel comfortable?"

G.H.

G. H. gives the first impression of being at ease with herself and her "place" in life, but there seems to be a deep sense of sadness in her countenance. She conducts herself well in political gatherings of ministers when she must, but, for the most part, she takes no part in them by choice. She does not see herself as an advocate or an adversary to any women's causes in ministry.

Her ministry has mainly been as an associate minister to male senior pastors, and for the most part these experiences have been positive. Rather than speak out when there is turmoil, she prefers to remain silent until things change with the passage of time. This eliminates the need to feel offended or mistreated in any way, she says, and she prefers not even to talk about women's issues for the most part. She has no ambition in the political system but prefers to remain where she is. In order to do this, she would prefer not to take part in anything that might associate her with the "feminist" movement.

I.J.

I. J. sees her greatest struggle as one of communication differences between her and male pastors. She sees men as more business like and task-oriented than she and is able to accept this for the most part with no problem. It bothers her that she is totally at the mercy of males as to salary and as to which jobs are hers, but to complain is too high a price to pay in order to keep her position secure. She certainly has faced discrimination as a female clergy person, but "when I get my head together and figure out what they (male clergy) want, I don't have any more problems." "If I just act right, it's okay," she says. If she does something exceptionally well, she knows that the males with whom she has served will not be happy about it for a period of time. She stated that she feels that the burden of making the relationships work is always on her shoulders, but she accepts this situation.

K.L.

K. L. is a male pastor who reports that he has worked well with female colleagues. He said, however, that he is of the old school where the "brotherhood" is very important. He stated that he would choose his male colleagues over his female colleagues if there was a close call. He wishes that the female clergy could just accept that premise and form their own network. He stated that he thinks that male clergy will remain in the power positions, and those few important positions which women do hold are at the mercy of the male who is the ultimate power in the conference. He stated that he feels secure in that situation but realizes that female clergy may not unless they have a male senior pastor who will protect them. "It's all in how you say it that makes the difference in success and failure," he says, "and most of the time women just don't say it right."

M.N.

M. N. has served in several ministerial positions. As we talked I got the sense that she has had her share of disappointments concerning her appointments within the conference; however, she left me with the feeling that she was still glad to be in the ordained ministry of the Church.

In the beginning of our conversation we talked about her overall perception of the appointive system of the United Methodist Church. One of the issues that seemed important to her concerned the opportunities for clergywomen to serve. During her time as an ordained person, she said that the opportunities for women to be the pastor-in-charge of a church were few and far between. Even though the women had the same education and even the same experience, their appointments were never as significant as their male colleagues with the same education and experience, she stated.

Another issue that seemed important to her was the way that women clergy are treated in the overall structure of an annual conference. She indicated that women had the same status as other minorities. By this she was saying that no one would say that women should not be in ministry because that would identify that person as a sexist. Given the current situation, it is not good to be labeled as someone who is against a minority group. Therefore, M. N. stated that the bigotry and sexism that is a part of an annual conference has to be more covert. Covert sexism is much harder to detect and prove, and so the plight of women clergy is difficult to bring to light.

When she was asked about the issue of justice and communication, she responded by saying she does not believe that there is any real justice at this time within an annual conference or perhaps even in society at large. She did seem to indicate that communication between male and female clergy is something that needs to be addressed. For her, communication could be an important ingredient that would help. She believes that if there could be some open honest communication, some of the problems now confronting clergywomen might be dealt with in a constructive way.

O.P.

O. P. is a mature professional person in every respect and would be seen as such in any setting. I set up an appointment with her, and in the midst of a sentence, she looked down at her watch and told me that the time which she had allotted to me was up without having informed me ahead of time that she had a limited amount of time for the appointment. I immediately had to identify a personal bias which I have about the importance of the pastoral, nurturing role of all persons in ministry. At this moment I did not see her as pastoral in any sense of the word, but I had to accept that that was my issue rather than hers.

I began by posing question number five concerning discrimination and asked her to elaborate on her own experience. A torrent of venom poured out not usually associated with women or with clergy. It was directed both toward her male colleagues as well as toward her female colleagues in ministry. Her language was filled with negative sexual overtones. The system had not been good to her while active in it, she stated. It was her opinion that justice issues for women in ministry are a lost cause, because neither male nor female clergy are willing to admit that there is a problem. "How can you work to correct something to which you do not admit existence?" she posed.

Q.R.

Q. R. is an ordained elder in full connection in the United Methodist Church and has served in more than one annual conference. He has served as both a solo pastor of a church and as a senior pastor of a church with multiple staff.

As our conversation began concerning the issue of women clergy in the conference, he appeared to be somewhat reserved in his comments. He seemed to be uncomfortable with the subject in general. I asked what he thought about women in ordained ministry. His reply was that the Discipline of the United Methodist Church provided for the ordination of women. That seemed like a way of skirting the intent of my question, so I probed a little deeper. He said that his experience with women in ministry was not positive. As we talked further, he said that women approached ministry differently than he did and that he was not comfortable with their style. When pressed, he responded by saying that the women clergy with whom he had been in contact seemed to lack the kind of energy he thought was necessary for being in ministry. Still I pressed him, and he responded further by saying that women clergy seemed to place their own personal concerns ahead of the concerns of the church they were serving. I asked him what priority the church had in his life, and his response was that it took first priority.

Another problem to which he alluded concerned women clergy and their use of positions of power. He referred to a woman within an annual conference where he had served whom he perceived as having a powerful position as a "power-hungry woman." I asked him if a man occupied the same position, would he say the same about him, and he said he did not know. What he felt about women in the system and their seeking of positions of power was that they still needed some experience before actually being appointed or selected to serve in the power positions of the conference.

Footnotes

47   The fourth aspect we probe is how an organization itself functions as an active addict. ... ...the characteristics of addiction in organizations as evidenced in communication, gossip, fear, isolation, dishonesty, supressed feelings, sabotage, projection, disrespect, confusion, control, denial, forgetfulness, self-centeredness, dualism, grandiosity, and planning as a form of control. Anne Wilson Schaef & Diane Fassel, The Addictive Organization. (New York: Harper San Francisco, 1988), p. 8.

48   All systems call for behaviors and processes from those within the system that are consistent with the system. Systems subtly and explicitly reward people for exhibiting these behaviors. Ibid., Schaef & Fassel, pp. 58-60.

49   I could see the positive effects of associations with family members when I asked a man who was very highly placed in his organization why he was particularly interested in making sure that women got a fair shake in his organization. He said it was because he had two daughters. "When I saw them coming up at their job," he said, " I realized they weren't playing on a level field." Tannen, Talking From 9 to 5. (New York: William Morrow and Company, Inc., 1994), pp. 216-217.

50   As these men perceive things, the women talk constantly, and it takes them five times as long to get through any conversation as it would take a similar group of men. They perceive the women's speech as less logical, less informed (except on "women's" subjects that don't interest men anyway), and more emotional, than their own. Suzette Haden Elgin, Ph.D., Genderspeak, (New York: John Wiley & Sons, Inc., 1993),pp. 278-279.

51   The problem with crying is...that a person who is crying can't talk... . Being unable to talk means being unable to defend yourself or negotiate—it means being helpless. Ibid., pp. 275-276.

52   The capacity to engage in an open, mutually empathic relational process rests on the maintenance of fluid "ego boundaries" ...and the capacity to be responsive and "moved" by the thoughts, perceptions, and feeling states of the other person. Op. cit., Jordan, et. al., p.167.

53   It is not surprising then that a subordinate group resorts to disguised and indirect ways of acting and reacting. While these actions are designed to accommodate and please the dominant group, they often, in fact, contain hidden defiance and "put ons." Jean Baker Miller, M.D. toward a new psychology of women, Second Edition. (Boston: Beacon Press, 1986), pp. 9-10.

54   The role of peacemaker reflects the general tendency among women to seek agreement. Deborah Tannen, Ph.D. You Just Don't Understand,. (New York: Valentine Books, 1990), pp. 167-168.

55   Women are taught that their main goal in life is to serve others—first men, and later, children. Op. cit., Miller, p. 62.

56   ...since those who do ask are judged less capable. Yet it seems that many women who are more likely than men to ask questions...are unaware that they may make a negative impression at the same time that they get information. Op. cit., Tannen, p. 27.

57   For most AME-speaking men, anything that involves negotiation, and that is not literally a matter of life or death, is a game. Op. cit., Elgin, p. 45.

58   It may be that some people have a gut-level, not-logically-thought-out sense that women should get less, either because they are expected to have lower abilities, or because they do not display their abilities, or because their rank and salaries are being measured against those of other women rather than their male peers. Op. cit., Tannen, Talking from 9 to 5., pp. 31-32.

59   Op. Cit., Schama, p. 92.

60   ...there is the observation that among those men whose lives have served as the model for adult development, the capacity for relationships is in some sense diminished and the men are constricted in their emotional expression. Relationships often are cast in the language of achievement, characterized by their success or failure, and impoverished in their affective range...Op. cit, Gilligan, p. 30.

61   Women are perhaps a little more polite in public; men are probably more concerned about moving things along as quickly as possible. Op. cit., Elgin, pp.166-167.

Chapter Five

The Shared Journey

A sharing in dialogue among clergy persons committed to better working relationships through communication between male and female clergy using Women's Growth in Connection.

Packing our Bag for the Journey

The first decision we had to make in carrying out our practicum was who and how many people would be invited to take part in the groups. One of our concerns was to try to gain access to as wide a spectrum of experience and age as possible from the clergy in the conference. We chose to limit our project to Anglo persons, because the African-American and Hispanic experience in issues of power and justice would complicate and broaden our project beyond the scope we felt prepared to accomplish. We, also, wanted to limit the group to no more than seven participants for issues of manageability.[62] As far as possible, Leta wanted to avoid inviting any person to be a part of her group who held a significant position of power over anyone else in the group in the appointive system of the designated church conference for study in this Project. This decision was based in part on the experience in the Brainstorming Group where the women participants had appeared to be fearful or at least "uncomfortable" in the presence of men and/or power. Because of the difficulty of finding enough women to participate in the group, Leta made one exception to her issue of power by inviting one person who was more vulnerable than others in the group because of her lack of tenure. The woman's fearful behavior and hesitancy to enter into full participation in the group proved to verify that the original decision to limit the group was correct. On the other hand, Tom chose to invite people who had a broad range of tenure, experience and authority in the chosen conference.

Another important decision we made which grew out of the brainstorming session was to divide the males and females into two separate groups because of the way the female clergy appeared to be intimidated by the presence of the male clergy. Despite our efforts to create a sense of security and guarantee anonymity, our system of appointment makes this almost impossible. There exists an incredible grapevine of information whereby everyone has worked in every other church or knows someone personally who has.

Leta extended the invitation to be a part of her group to 13 women who had served as associates to male pastors. (See Appendix #3a and #3b.) Out of the 13 invited, six responded positively. Of the other seven, one asked to come on a come-and-go basis, three expressed regrets (one does not work well in the mornings and two could not work it into their schedule), two did not respond at all, although one had asked specifically to be invited, one agreed to come and did not and one came for the third session only. In explanation of the latter two, one explained to Tom that she decided she did not want to be in a "controversial/negative" group (an opinion she formed without ever having attended), but she never explained this to Leta. The other person who appeared for one session only had experienced a crisis which prevented her from participating in the first two sessions. No explanation was ever given by her to the leader as to why she did not continue. One member of the group felt moved to make explanations for her. Of the six who participated fully, Leta had interviewed four, and two had participated in the Brainstorming group.

Tom decided to extend the invitation to be a part of his group to 20 Anglo clergymen, hoping to have no more than seven respond positively. (See Appendix #4a and #4b.) Those who were invited ranged in age from approximately 35 to 70 years of age and in tenure from probationary to retired membership status. Tom received back from those inquiries five positive responses.

Among the positive responses there was one who was not in full-connection, one with less than 10 years' tenure in full membership, two with 10 to 20 years', and one who was retired with many years tenure in full membership. A letter was sent out to those who had responded positively with notice of the proposed dates, time and meeting place for our study group, and everything was made ready for the first meeting of the male clergy study group.

During the several years in which Leta has been concentrating on reading and examining feminist literature and teaching courses using that same literature and discussing this with both male and female colleagues, the book, Women's Growth in Connection (Writings from the Stone Center) emerged as the prototypical literature to use for our groups. We found that this book was being used in mixed pastoral counseling groups within the geographical confines of the conference in which we were carrying out our project. We arranged for the participants to buy the book at a discount at a local bookstore and ordered a sufficient number for use.

What we considered to be a rather insignificant factor in the process, that of choosing a place to hold our sessions, proved to be a very important piece of information for our study. We wanted central places for those who agreed to be part of the groups. Leta called two large churches with no thought that she would be turned down and was refused a place in one of the churches and told that she would have to change meeting rooms every time she met at the other church. The third church which she approached offered her a place after commenting, "Oh, you are leading that radical group of feminists!" At this point the issue of anonymity and security of the participants took on much more significance than we had previously considered it to have. [63] On the other hand, Tom had no difficulty at all.

Another issue involved meeting times. We decided to hold six sessions two weeks apart and gave the participants the opportunity to choose the most convenient time and day of the week prior to holding the first session. We communicated this by mail. After holding our first session, Tom's group chose to readjust the six dates to meet their various schedules. Leta's group chose to stay with the six presented dates because no alternative dates could be found to accommodate everyone. It was at this point that Leta's group decided not to allow anyone to participate on a come-and-go basis. In effect they chose to be a closed group. [64]

Tom chose to utilize prepared questions based on the assigned readings. The questions were designed to help elicit dialogue from the group and to guide the discussion. Leta chose at each session to introduce one or two major questions from her reading to which some response could be made.

It was not possible within the six weeks time frame to cover the entire book, Women's Growth in Connection. We, therefore made the arbitrary decision before we ever held the first session as to which chapters to choose for discussion, while at the same time encouraging the participants to read the entire book. The chapters selected for discussion involved varying themes centering around a woman's sense of self, mutuality and women at work. Chosen subjects for discussion will be listed as the sessions are discussed in detail.

Unpacking the Bag in Anticipation of the Continuing Journey

We both arrived early for our first sessions in order to preview the
rooms where we would be meeting and to have time to adjust to the
space and prepare ourselves mentally for the experience that awaited
us. There were similarities in our reaction to the meeting space in that
we both felt a sense of emptiness and began immediately to arrange the
furniture so that we could create a sense of community. Tom arranged
folding chairs and a portion of a sectional sofa roughly into a square.
Leta took parts of a sectional sofa and arranged them in a circle in one
small corner of the large room. Tom's room was very centrally
located within the church building giving a view to the outside;
whereas, Leta's was on the second floor of the building where no
interruption of any kind was possible and no view to the outside.[65]

All but one of Tom's group arrived at the appointed hour.
Approximately 15 minutes was spent exchanging pleasantries allowing
time for the remaining member to arrive. He never did and never
responded until a letter with revised meeting dates was sent out (See
appendix 4c). At that time he replied that he would not be able to
participate. Three of Leta's group arrived on time, and one arrived
about 20 minutes late, which she was to do consistently. According to
Irvin D. Yalom, this signifies resistance.[66]   One arrived 40 minutes
late because she had gone to the wrong church by mistake. One of the
group who had arrived on time left after 20 minutes to attend a
required conference related meeting which she had been ordered not to
miss. One member was very uncomfortable and expressed that this
discomfort was related to her fears of being associated with a radical
group.

The men in Tom's group chose to sit on the sofa rather than in the
folding chairs and consistently sat in the same seat each session.
Tom chose to sit on the floor rather than sit on a folding chair which
would have put him opposite the other men and in a higher physical
position than they were. Leta's group simply sat in the closest open
space as they arrived, and Leta was part of the circle. With the
exception of one member who chose to sit on Leta's left, there was
never any order as to where the women sat.

The initial time was spent discussing ground rules in both groups.
Both Leta and Tom proposed the possibility of recording the
conversations. Tom's group had no difficulty agreeing to this but saw
no need to sign a release. Leta's group unanimously decided that they
did not want the sessions to be recorded. Confidentiality was stressed
even to the point of not revealing the participants of each group to the
other group, although each group knew that there was a group of the
opposite gender meeting with similar study material which would

contribute to a Doctor of Ministry study project.

All but one of Tom's group had acquired the book and prepared for the session. The one who did not have the book never did avail himself of it and thus was not prepared for the sessions. All but one of Leta's group had bought the book, but all had not always read it in preparation for the session. The one member who never bought the book continued to affirm that she was in the process of getting it. It never "arrived," and thus she was never prepared ahead of time for the discussion. This person was also the one who consistently arrived a little late. Discussion in both groups was always animated, and one of Leta's group voiced the affirmation that the study book had impacted her life in a way like no other book had with the exception of the Bible.

When explanations were made in Tom's group as to how the participants were chosen and the fact that two groups were running at the same time based on gender, the men requested that they be allowed to meet in a joint session with the women, preferably the final session. Because of the need for confidentiality, Tom said that it might not be possible. Leta checked with her group, and they chose not to meet with the men. It should be noted that Leta was in agreement with this based on her experience in the Brainstorming session.

Leta began by explaining to her group her difficulty in finding a place to meet in an effort to help the women understand that more significance was being placed on the purpose of the group than she had anticipated by the male senior pastors of the large churches she approached. She explained that she had viewed the group as "just another opportunity for spiritual growth" which would have the end result of affirming women in ministry. The women in the group were; however, not surprised at all at the male senior pastors' response. Some had heard that the word was out to keep radical groups from meeting in United Methodist churches.

The readings for our first session were chapters 1 and 5: "A Developmental Perspective" and "The Meaning of Mutuality."

Tom: Our discussion began with two of the members of my group pointing out that the book we were studying was from Wellesley College. I had wanted to open up our time together by allowing the members of the group to talk about their overall impressions of the chapters they had read. There was a remark by one member that in the beginning he felt somewhat defensive, because he felt that the focus of the book might take on the characteristic of male-bashing. He went on to say that he felt that many of the points that were made were on target and he found himself agreeing with the authors concerning the need for the self to be in relationship. The two who knew Wellesley

College explained that their own stereotypical thinking associated this college with radical feminism and they were apprehensive about the journey we were about to take.

Our conversation moved along the lines of the way that boys are raised and are steered away from showing empathy. The group felt that this was no longer an applicable statement to the way that boys are raised today, and that pastors are certainly the exception to the rule.

Another point brought to light dealt with the way men share with one another when women are not present and how this differs when women appear on the scene. The men felt that the author's evaluation that men never share with one another was not accurate.

The next major issue had to do with the fact that men, even while sharing with one another, operate from a competitive mode while women always "tell their stories" from a relational aspect. They stated that they believed that with women there is no effort to problem-solve; whereas, men do this in a competitive spirit. There was one dissenting voice where one member felt that women cut off the competitive aspect of men's conversation.

A question arose as to the ultimate goal of the group. "Was the intent to make the men present adopt feminine ways of relating?" asked the men. I explained that the goal was to heighten the sensitivity of both the male and female group members to the different ways in which we communicate both in word and action in an effort to transform the Church so that justice might be available to all.

Our group moved on to a discussion of the issue of power and how power affects the way males and females communicate. The final comment made by one member was to the effect that he never felt safe unless his supervisor was a white male brought about complete agreement by all the other males present. The fact that Tom posed the question as to how women and other marginalized people must feel always having to accept supervision from someone different than they, elicited a brief response.

Leta: One member volunteered to begin our discussion by presenting the issue which touched her the most deeply: "naming our gifts." This related to a woman's need to be connected and the role of servanthood. She pointed out that preaching is an activity which affirms authority and one of the most important activities of the pastor, but during the time of preaching and affirming of authority, the member felt that she was disconnected from the congregation. All agreed that women fear this sense of disconnection, but they do not want to give up the right to preach. One of the members of the group never felt this sense of disconnection, because she is a story-teller and she feels that the congregation journeys with her throughout the sermon and never disconnects. The question was asked if men, not valuing connection as much as women, ever accept the servanthood role that a pastor is asked to live-out. No one attempted to answer the question.

The conversation turned to the issue of the political activity in the conference in which they all serve and how it is based on rules that men learn from early childhood. It was agreed that women are not socialized to "play the game," and, further, it was not even felt by most of the women to be a desirable way to function. It interferes with a woman's need of and value for relationships, being connected. The way that some have dealt with this problem is just to "shut down." "Shutting down" appears to mean severing all interconnectedness in the political process of the conference.

The women brought up the fact that often their greatest criticism of the way they carry out ministry in the church comes from women parishioners who have been trained to evaluate ministry according to the rules set up by men. Even the most caring pastoral acts, such as long visits to parishioners in the hospitals, are criticized as inappropriate when they are carried out by women.

It was pointed out that there are specific tasks for which women have not been considered, such as starting up a new church. An example was given of a woman who proposed to her supervisor the opening of a new church. The proposal was rejected. The reason given for not appointing the woman was first of all that she did not fit the model of the conference for the kind of person who does new church start-ups. When pressed, her supervisor said that her skills were much too pastoral to fit the energy demanded in a new church start-up. Continuing this conversation, the members of the group felt that part of the ground women are breaking in the conference is in redefining the various roles of ministry in the Church. For example, there had never been a female minister of evangelism in a large church before two years ago. The minister of evangelism was seen as a young white male "on his way up." Once the role was successfully filled by a female, other appointments to this role in other large churches took place. One member brought up the fact that a new church start-up falls under the same category as minister of evangelism and is associated with a young white male "on his way up;" however, it was remarked that a woman had been assigned to do a new church start-up, and the project failed. The response of the group was that this woman and the church were set up to fail, because she was not the right person, the location was inappropriate and the congregation was saddled with a large debt from the beginning. Thus, women in ministry were given a set-back because that failure to perform in a specific way by one woman will always be used as an example of the inability of all women to do a new church start-up.

As the women began to part, one member mentioned that this discussion brought out a lot of intense feeling. To this remark another responded, "Perhaps the male ministers were right, and we are a subversive group."

Second Session
Our second session dealt with chapters 8, 9 and 10: "The Meanings of "Dependency" in Female-Male Relationships," "Relationship and Empowerment" and "The Construction of Anger in Women and Men."

Tom: When I arrived at the second session, all those members who had been present at the first session were there. I informed the group that one person who previously had planned to be with us would not be joining us. There was no response to this news.

One of the members began the discussion by saying that after he had read the material he had to wonder whether or not the authors were living in the real world. He did not believe that the world could operate without the issue of power coming into play. Another member reminded the group that the authors were a part of a Wellesley study group, and that although he did not mean that derogatorily, that was a distinction of which he was clearly reminded. He continued by saying that the feminist agenda was apparent and that it was a bit off-balance, that the authors were not operating in the real world and that they were out of touch with how women operate in the Church as opposed to society in general. He pointed out that the authors, by their own admission, were struggling to find new language and vocabulary to express what is so uniquely female. It is his understanding that the United Methodist Church operates with a collective interaction and collegiality in relationship to other people as a process for community growth, and that these authors apparently had no concept of what the United Methodist Church was all about. Our conversation then picked up on the issue of anger. One of the members said that anger really was not an emotion with which they were comfortable. Several members of the group said that anger was okay to express but that they felt that it was inappropriate to focus too much attention on anger.

I wanted the group to explain to me what was meant by too much attention. The consensus seemed to be that when anger itself is allowed to be the primary issue discussed rather than what causes the anger, then that is too much attention. Basically, they were tired of women talking about anger and not taking any positive steps to eradicate it. They saw such conversation as non-productive.

I pushed for the members to discuss the right of women to express their anger, and I asked what they meant by productive. Productive seemed to mean finding solutions. As far as the right of women to express anger, the group agreed that just expressing anger served no real purpose when there was work to be done.

I asked the group to help me differentiate between how they feel when Anglo men express anger, since all the group is Anglo, and how they feel when women or minority group members express anger. They all agreed that they feel greater tension when the latter express anger, but they are accustomed to and accepting of Anglo men's expression of anger. Anglo men are trained from childhood to compete, and competition seems always to involve anger.

The discussion could have continued, but our allotted time was over and the conversation had dwindled down.

Leta: All the members of the group were present for this second session. One of the members arrived late apologizing for not having the book. This made the group a bit uncomfortable. Pleasantries and news of the conference were exchanged.

One member brought up the subject of trust. Feeling that her male senior pastor did not trust her after a year of working with him, she finally confronted him with this issue. His response was that he had not trusted her until that moment. She asked of the group some feedback on this matter. The group felt that it was when she became confrontive, which is understood to be a male characteristic born of their competitive upbringing, that he understood her. The group saw the issue as a matter of communication. The person who posed the question shared the fact that confronting her superior was extremely difficult because she had been reared to believe that "this is a man's world and that she had better learn her submissive role well." One of the members inquired of her as to whether she was really talking about trust or about empowerment. Her response was that she had had two situations serving as an associate, one where the senior pastor trusted her, the second where the senior pastor did not. She saw the issue, therefore as trust, because the one who did not trust her, flagrantly used his power over her. Two in the group saw this as a gender issue, where some males were more trusting of females than others.

The conversation then turned to empowerment in the Church as opposed to the secular world. One member, a second career person, expressed that there was much more equal treatment in the secular world than in the Church. Another member, who was also a second career person, disagreed. In her first profession there were some very clearly defined rules as to which ladders were open to success between males and females within a given discipline. Those disciplines open to the males had a higher salary potential.

One of the women had called the "guru" of the conference in her particular specialty to ask his advice about a very serious matter which she was facing in her local church. The "guru" in this instance is a male whom she perceived as immediately putting her in a subordinate role rather than treating her as a colleague. This made her angry, and, by recognizing and affirming her feelings of anger, she was able to handle the situation and to bring it to a positive conclusion. The consensus of the group was to remember that positions of power in the Church need to be run by God and not by people.

Another member of the group pointed out that she was raised in a family where no one could show anger or express any negative thoughts. She, therefore, had to learn how to show anger as an adult. Some of the group felt that affirming anger and showing anger were two different things. No consensus was reached. The discussion on anger moved on to a discussion of the way that some senior pastors treated the women in the group who served as their associates, such as not recognizing their need for a day off or time away from the church. The group felt that this could be viewed simply as an associate issue, but it was also brought up that for a woman this poses the problem of being in two subordinate positions at the same time. One is subordinate as an associate but one is also subordinate as a woman because a woman by virtue of the fact that she is female, is not always recognized as a pastor.

To illustrate this issue one of the members told about her experience of serving as an associate in charge of taking in new members to the church. When she took a couple who were new members back to the room to register them, she expressed her delight and surprise that they had joined without informing her ahead of time. The minister was still fully robed and was wearing her clerical stole and had been a part of the leadership team in worship service. The response of the wife in the couple was of surprise. She exclaimed, "Why, I did call you last week and tell you that we were going to join. You're Dr. Jim's secretary, aren't you?" Being woman made her invisible as a pastor. The group member who related this story remembered reading about a similar situation in Deborah Tannen's book, Talking from 9 to 5, where Dr. Tannen was mistaken for a secretary by a female student when there could not have been any doubt that she was a professor because of where she was sitting behind her desk in her office.

Another issue that was brought up during this session dealt with the fact that some senior pastors often hold part-time secular jobs leaving their associates to carry greater loads. There was unanimous agreement that female clergy must work 1 1/2 times harder to be accepted than do the male clergy.

This led to the discussion that male pastors are taken care of by their female parishioners; whereas, female pastors are not. Examples are given of male pastors who are widowed whose female parishioners bring them food and of all the nurturing, cleaning-up duties that female parishioners do for male pastors that they do not do in churches pastored by female clergy. Some congregations make it clear that they keep salaries high in order to avoid having a female pastor, knowing that women in this conference are never considered for churches in the higher salary range.

Knowing the battle for acceptance by the Church of the validity of a woman's call to ministry some of the group suggested that opting-out was not such a bad idea. At the least, it would reduce the pain for the individual clergywoman. One member suggested that all that we had done would be forgotten to which another responded, "Who wants to be remembered?" Another member suggested that it is only in being remembered that we will help those who follow us which is a tenet of all liberation movements.

A tremendous surge of feeling was brought forth in the group as one member shared a story of the rape of an 80 year old, very active female parishioner and of the male senior pastor's questioning whether or not the rape was her fault. The group lamented the fact that they did not find the pastors, including some female pastors, of the Church to be intentional in their caring for others and in justice issues. They found them quicker to seek blame rather than to try to bring about change in the system that would foster justice. Deep pain was voiced about the fact that no real effort was being put forth by the majority of the pastors now serving churches to understand women's special issues. The group felt that women bring the gift of themselves and of their own special upbringing that could bring about the needed revolution in the Church. "Is this what Jesus was about?" they asked.

The discussion became heated as the time drew to an end. One member voiced the thought, "Why try to bring about change in an institution which is dying?" Everyone echoed, "Let's start with that next week!"

Third Session
This third session was devoted to chapter 11: "Women and Power."

Tom: The session began by discussing our own definitions of power, with one member's pointing out his resonance with the author's definition of power, "the ability to make a change." I interjected that I thought the author had also said that power was the ability to empower someone else, to bring them along and enhance their power. The first person replied to the effect that the Church has tried to say that we as clergy persons have the power to make changes when indeed we choose to build a sense of power around ourselves rather than allowing God to make that change. I reminded the group of how we use power in worship and suggested what it might be like for us to step away from the role of being a leader in worship and to become a prompter rather than a leader. That would open the way for God to lead, and we agreed that it is God who has the power.

Our discussion was guided toward the different ways that men and women view power and use it differently. One member of the group suggested that men are going to use power as a tool to bring about change and further their own goals but that women would probably not see power as something to be used by an individual but as something to be used to empower a whole group or community of persons. In response to this, one member of the group said that the men's use of power is realistic; whereas, women's use of power is like "pie-in-the-sky." I queried as to whether we should dismiss this definition or try to understand it. It was felt that the present system leaves the possibility for abuse, therefore, could use some understanding.

Some in the group suggested that women do know how to form caucuses or to lobby for increased awareness of issues. The members feel that the ability to do this is important in our annual and general conferences. I suggested it would appear that this ability has not brought about appreciable change for individual women, and it may simply say that women have learned to play by the rules made by men.

Somebody suggested that women probably need to be more assertive in their interactions with congregations and with other clergy. I responded that this often causes more pain than pleasure, for they are then called names that rhyme with witch; whereas, men are seen as strong leaders for the same behavior. There was some disagreement among the group members but it was admitted that women have a very fine line to walk in claiming and using power.

The group discussed the issue of the loneliness women probably feel when they claim and use power. They agreed that there is a certain "aloneness" that occurs whenever one climbs the ladder in a hierarchical organization. One person expressed belief that the utilization of power does not necessarily cut off the relationship with others, but another person suggested that since women are a minority in the structure of the conference, those who were chosen for positions of power would be set apart from their sisters in ministry.

The group in general agreed that those who hold power cannot be in close relationship with those over whom they hold power. Some expressed regret that the situation is like that.

I asked the group if any of them felt threatened by women who appear to be powerful. One member said that he felt threatened when anyone who was "different" from him held power over him. Not all members of the group admitted that they did not feel threatened by a woman having some power. When I pressed them on their having stated a woman, rather than women, they agreed that as long as the woman who held some power was still in the minority, they did not feel too threatened. There was some discussion among the group as to how they would respond to what they perceived as a negative use of power by a woman, and one member said that as long as there were men in power who outnumbered the women in power, males really have nothing to fear.

Leta: For this third session two of the group members were absent. One had informed the group at our last session that she would not be present this time. This meeting was unusual due to the presence of a woman who had been invited to join and had been unable to attend the first two sessions due to various reasons. There was the usual sharing of news with particular attention to what was going on in the life of the new member to the group. This new member took a very active and verbal part in the discussion, and all seemed genuinely happy to have her with us. After a very animated discussion about, "Women and Power," where one member had contributed little, that very member commented that she had gotten a totally different meaning from the chapter under discussion than the rest of us had. She finds that when she does get power, she botches it "big time" because of hearing what her mother taught her as a child that "this is a man's world" where women are submissive and should never have power. An older member of the group's understanding of power was that one never sees it as misused if one is willing to see God working through every appointment within the system as she has been able to discern in her own life. Several of the members of the group reacted strongly to this understanding of power. Their feeling was that women accept abuse in the system by writing it off as "God's will."

An example was given of an interaction of one of the group members with a very respected male clergy member of the conference. While discussing the use of power between men and women, he became extremely agitated and said that women are too aggressive and that if women ever do get power, he fears that men will revolt against them.

One of the group members compared power to our efforts at self-differentiation and stated that we must all accept that it is everyone's right to self-differentiate. We are fighting for the right to choose, according to her. We must be open to dialogue if we ever hope to change.

In looking back over the session's discussion, it appears that we returned over and over again to the issue of trust. One member reminded us that you only trust those who have proven themselves trustworthy. We closed with the words of a therapist to one of our members who said, "If someone betrays you once, 'shame on them.' If they betray you twice, 'shame on you.'"

Fourth Session

For the fourth session the study groups read chapters 12 and 13: "The "Self-in-relation": Implications for Depression," "Work Inhibitions in Women."

Tom: Two of our members were absent from this session, but our discussion was animated none-the-less. We began with talking about the different developmental paths that males and females follow. Given this information, I asked if it were possible for justice to prevail for women and men when they share the same working environment. One group member said that he believed that justice can be present if both men and women are willing to work toward the same understanding of justice. The other replied that he did not want to be pessimistic, but he did not believe that justice could actually be expected of all of the people all of the time. The other member wanted to press the issue and asked if the previous statement could be used as an excuse not even to try for equality and justice? We decided that it was important for males and females to be honest in their expectations of one another and in their perceptions of the work environment. The group hoped that this honesty would help both men and women see where they might be on target and where they still needed to do some work toward achieving justice.

One of the issues that I felt was important for the group to address this time concerned how women often take responsibility for failures in relationships. I related to the group a situation in this conference where a woman associate felt that her miscommunication with the male senior pastor was her failure properly to perceive a particular situation. One of the members stated that the same problem could arise with a male associate. I asked him if the male associate would take responsibility for the miscommunication? Probably not, was the member's response.

Our discussion moved to the issue of appointments. As we began to discuss the appointments that women receive in this conference, none of the members seemed to understand how the women could be disappointed in the progress that women have made. I related to them a story of two clergy, male and female, who entered the conference at the same time but who now have very different positions on the career ladder. The group agreed that both clergy were competent and had the skills necessary to pastor most churches in the conference. Still the group refused to acknowledge the disparity in their positions. According to the group, since females had only been in the appointive system a comparatively short time, they should not expect to hold the same kinds of appointments as their male counterparts despite their gifts for ministry. The consensus was that because women were still fairly new in the Church, it would take some time for them to gain the kinds of appointments that males hold. No consensus could be reached, and it was near time to leave, so we spent the last few minutes re-setting dates hoping to accommodate all the members.

Leta: Although one member had notified the group that she would be absent for this session, it turned out that only one member besides me was present. I offered her the opportunity to go on to work and suggested that we would try to work this reading into the next session. She chose not to leave, for the reading had had a powerful impact on her. She wanted to discuss it with me and to share her response to it, because it related very closely to her present position in ministry.

She had difficulty with a statement in the book that suggested that depression in women is a "normal" state because women are constantly being put down. It is not normal, according to the book, for women to be considered in need of therapy just because they are depressed. The member of the group felt that men are just as depressed as women. Her big issue for years has been working on "integration" in her life, and now it is difficult for her to switch to "connection." For me, this was not an issue, because I see women as born into and socialized into connection.

This member was also the one who expressed that she had had difficulty with sabotaging her own success. Despite various perceived successes, she says, she is always looking for someone who will find what it is that she did wrong.

This participant sees herself as invisible to those in power over her and cited several instances which illustrated that she has good reason to feel as she does. The situation is particularly poignant in the fact that the lay person in charge of her is female and appears to be the one who does her the most harm. I could relate to the story of the female who was harmful to her as the one in power over her, for the same situation had existed for me in a prior appointment.

In searching for help from a superior in the hierarchical system, the group member was more confused than ever and referred to her situation as "the female clergy dilemma." We wondered together if there is a way for women to find affirmation in ministry in any annual conference."

Fifth Session

For the fifth session we read chapter 15: "The Meaning of Care: Reframing Treatment Models."

Tom: When I arrived for the fifth session of the male clergy group, there was no one present. After a few minutes the pastor of the church where we hold our sessions and who is a member of the group came in. He apologized, saying that he had not read the assigned chapter and would be dependent on the others to lead the discussion. We waited for approximately 45 minutes, and no one else arrived. It seemed fruitless to attempt any discussion of the material.

I sent a letter after the fifth session to the members of the group expressing my regret for their having been absent. I asked the members to be prepared to discuss the readings for both sessions at our next meeting.

Leta: All members of the group were present with the exception of the one person who had only come for the third session. Although telephone calls were made and a note sent to her, no response was ever received as to why she did not return. One member who knew her better than most of us felt the need to explain her absence by saying that she had a late start and had experienced some difficulties in her life. All of our reading suggests that this is a normal reaction of women caring for one another.

The one member without the book explained again that she was in the process of getting her a copy. Since I had obtained a copy for a friend the week before, I was curious as to why an explanation had to be attempted. One member who had been well-prepared for three previous sessions, had not read either of the chapters from the week before that she missed nor the ones we were to discuss today.

Over half of the time set aside for the session was spent discussing a pending divorce of a male clergy colleague. Attention was paid to every detail that everyone could remember. Tannen speaks of this phenomenon among women as a way to gain status in our social network by knowing and sharing secrets. She says this differs from the way that men do this. Men "...gain status by their own accomplishments."[67]   It seemed that we would not be talking about any of the designated material for discussion, so I attempted to interject some of this material and get on with the designated task. Most of the group appeared offended when it was suggested that we drop the subject at hand. It seems that questions of, "Who was pastoring the wife?" and the role of the minister to the congregation, to the pastor, to anybody concerned was of consuming importance. One group member expressed her discomfort and left for the restroom. She had wanted to discuss the book, because it had greatly impacted her life.

Rather than go back to the discussion of the book, a very heated conversation began concerning a required event in which some members of the group had been participants. The difference in interpretation of the effectiveness of the event on the people's lives and the use or misuse of power seemed to be in direct correlation to those who felt they had no choice in the matter and those who thought it was purely voluntary. The same person who was extremely uncomfortable with the prior discussion and wanted to get on task also was insistent that the present subject matter was depressing and asked that it be dropped. I, personally, was very uncomfortable with our ignoring the assigned material, but I realized that the group interaction was powerful in its affirmation of the truths found in the book which we were sharing.

The member who felt urgently the need to discuss the designated material at hand began to present what she considered the most important thoughts of the reading. Another member stated immediately that she had a personal issue involving her work which she thought related to the discussion. The two seemed totally unrelated to me, but I felt it important to let the group go in the direction it seemed best at this time. The issue presented by the second member of the group had to do with justice. Her question to us was how she could make a stand for justice and not do great damage to her career. Several suggestions were given, but it was finally concluded that there was no way that she could stand for what she thought was justice and not harm herself irreparably in the political system of the conference.

We returned to the first designated topic for discussion which had to do with closeness, often called community or connectedness. It seems that a certain male senior pastor has voiced his desire to the congregation that he does not want closeness and he does not want feedback. The congregation has accepted this. The problem arises because the female associate needs closeness and feedback. How does she handle this without hurting her position? It was felt that she simply needed to voice her need for community and to stress that it was her need which she was asking to be met and not anyone else's. One member of the group pointed out that building close relationships can be a detriment, because the community builds around that person and follows them always, if not in body, then in spirit.

One member of the group reported that a study done at a certain theological seminary had revealed that 90% of the female students had been sexually abused as children. No one seemed amazed. I queried as to how many male students of the seminary could have been abused if a similar questionnaire had been administered to them.

One person had to leave a bit early because of a meeting which would involve a lot of stress. I asked the group to have a moment of silence for her, and if they wanted to pray, to do so. There was silence. No one prayed out loud. I closed with, "Amen." Two of the people stayed to talk after we left.

N.B. A letter was sent to all participants after the fifth session reminding them of the final session. (See appendices 5a and 5b.)

Sixth Session

Chapter 17 was discussed during the final session: "Empathy, Mutuality and Therapeutic Change: Clinical Implications of a Relational Model.

Tom: For the final session everyone was present and on time.

We began immediately with some discussion of the material from the fifth session from which everyone was absent. The conversation centered on whether or not women needed to conform to the male model of ministry in order to be considered successful and competent. One member stated that most clergy persons operate on their own individual styles of ministry. Most of the group decided that since ministry is modeled in different ways by clergy that there is no one model that could be assessed as being THE model.

Another issue that arose from our discussions was the ability to develop close caring relationships with female parishioners and female clergy colleagues. Two of the males called to the group's attention the fact that fear exists among the male clergy based on the prevalence of sexual misconduct cases that have been filed against male clergy in recent times. No one was willing to say that it was wrong for the misconduct cases to be filed. They only bemoaned the fact that as a result, they did not feel free to initiate or maintain close relationships with female colleagues as they had done in the past. The members of the group reported that they knew many colleagues in ministry who were now refusing to engage in counseling with parishioners of the opposite sex. Because of the need for privacy and confidentiality that is a necessary part of the counseling relationship, the group felt that they were exceedingly vulnerable to charges against which they may not be able to defend themselves.

I asked the group if they believed that female clergy persons were better equipped to do counseling with women than their male counterparts. One of the members said that he did believe that women probably would respond better to a female clergy person in counseling. One of the reasons given was that females may tend to be better at empathizing with those whom they counsel, thereby giving them the appearance of genuine concern. It is the nurturing side of females that the group member was referring to. Another member said that he believed it was only a matter of time before female clergy persons may have to fear sexual misconduct charges being filed against them.

Most of the group agreed that they try to be sensitive to the ways that females perceive themselves and the world around them. Several members said that they believed that this was probably a key ingredient to bridging the communication gap between male and female clergy persons. One member stated that he believed that this kind of sensitivity needed to be a "two-way street" in order for there to be any real change.

When asked, most of the group agreed that in time female clergy would achieve the same status and opportunities that their male counterparts now enjoy. One of the members referred the group to the large numbers of female clergy who are in the seminaries and coming before the boards of ordained ministry. It was suggested that there would soon be a time when the numbers of male and female clergy would be equal in the conference. I asked if this prospect would be frightening to the members of the group. No one said that it would.

As I moved the group toward some closure, I asked if anyone had learned anything in the study group which would change their way of relating to female clergy or to females in general. There was some general agreement that the study had provided new understanding of women but that some of what they had read still seemed to be too radical to be taken seriously. One member said that the group study had provided him with some insight into the plight of female clergy and that he hoped he would be better equipped to relate to his female colleagues in the future. There was, also, some regret expressed at not having had the opportunity to meet with the female study group. I again reminded them of the fear that the women in the other group had concerning anonymity. The group as a whole believed that valuable learning could only take place when they were given that opportunity to interact with others of like mind. This, he said, involved risk which is a necessary element for growth. Until there is open and honest dialogue between the male and female clergy persons of this conference, he insisted, the issues of justice and equality cannot be addressed.

I thanked the members for their participation in the group and asked if any of them had considered sharing what they had learned in other groups. No one seemed to want to start a group utilizing the material we had studied; however, they hoped to introduce some of the ideas into other groups of which they are already a part.

Leta: The entire group was present for our final session.

No one could say that this chapter was of any particular benefit to them, but one member mentioned that the part on how we must take care of ourselves was one she had learned well before she answered her call to ministry. Because of this learning, she then felt badly during her Clinical Pastoral Education period at a local hospital. At that time she had to think in terms of taking care of others and often found herself crying for them. I mentioned that I had spent my life taking care of others and I was now learning to take care of myself.

We mentioned the models we had had as children—those where we were always urged to think of others. For example, "Clean your plate. There are children starving in China." The examples did not make sense.

One member of the group brought up the fact that we are to love our neighbor as ourselves which tells us that we must, indeed, love ourselves. She told about how she does what she feels is good for herself, what she enjoys, and she does not feel pressure to do what the conference hierarchy demands that she do. She continued with an example of a female clergy person who is taking some drastic measures in order to fulfill the conference expectations of her. These actions may prove harmful to her and her family, but to do otherwise in her thinking would damage her progress up the career ladder. One member of the group felt uncomfortable discussing a person who was not present and asked that the discussion end. I reminded the one who had told the story that it is always important to take into consideration the different situations in which we live and move and have our being.

One person in our group shared the concern that as a female clergy person who is a member of an otherwise all-male study group, she often has higher expectations placed on her participation than the male members do. It has even been pointed out to her that she is considered different.

In discussing inequalities existing in the conference the conversation quickly returned to a subject which had occupied our attention during the last session. The subject centered on whether or not we should be involved in counseling our parishioners. There are differing opinions. It seems that some supervisors have told pastors that they must not do counseling with their parishioners. If they do counsel them, they would not be able to preach for fear of revealing confidences. We asked, "How can we preach if we do not know our people?"

I asked the group how the book and the group had helped them. The answers were: "I loved the group and its small size." "The book was the best I have ever read outside the Bible, and it has changed my life." "It changed my life as well." "I need a group with whom I can dialogue made up of women who have some understanding of who I am."

I urged the group to form other similar groups in the hope that in understanding each other, we would be better prepared to work for the justice of all within the conference, both male and female. This commitment would not only be for the good of the women clergy and those parishioners whom we serve, but also for the salvation of the male clergy among us. I remembered reading an article while returning home from a Shalom Conference and being filled with a desire for wholeness. The article told of Archbishop Tutu in South Africa who wept for the oppressor as well as the oppressed, for he knew that in the core of the oppressor's being he suffers just as those whom he oppresses.[68]

One of the group members asked to be notified if another similar group ever formed. No one actually said that they would initiate a new group.

After thanking them for participating in this group, we all left the room with what I felt might be a certain sense of let-down or sadness that we would not meet again as a group.

Footnotes

62   ...the ideal size of an ineractional therapy group is approximately seven, with an acceptable range of five to ten members. Irvin D. Yalom, The Theory and Practice of Group Psychotherapy. (New York: Basic Books, Inc., Publishers, 1970), p. 215.

63   I have seen many a valuable discussion stem from the concern about confidentiality which touches such areas as trust, shame, fear of disclosure, or degree of commitment to the group. Ibid., pp. 120-121.

64   At their inception groups are designated by their leader as open or closed: a closed group, once begun, closes its gates, accepts no new members, and meets usually for a predetermined number of sessions... . Ibid., p. 209.

65   See "The Physical Setting," Ibid., p. 208.

66   Tardiness and irregular attendance usually signify resistance to therapy and should be regarded in the same way in which one regards these phenomena in individual therapy. Ibid., pp. 245-246.

67   Op. cit., Tannen, Talking 9 to 5, pp. 154-155.

68   Archbishop Desmond Tutu, Interview. (Dallas/Fort Worth, Texas: American Airlines Magazine, October 1, 194), p. 154.

Chapter Six

Reflecting Upon
the Journey

Is the journey over?

In this final section of our project we will attempt both to evaluate and to conclude our discussion by recalling the different areas we have broached. Intertwined with this reflection there will be remarks that are intended to lift up some of the valuable learning that has taken place for both of us. Amidst these remarks we will also share the most important recommendations as well as suggestions for future research and journeys into liberation and justice, especially as they relate to the interaction between female and male clergy persons.

Tom: In considering our theological rationale do you think, Leta, that we have failed in any way to cover the subject of justice and women in ministry?

Leta: One of the major learnings for me in this area is the discovery of the ignorance of or perhaps lack of interest in reading Scripture with an eye toward what it says about God's intent in creation and Jesus' life and witness to and for women. It could be that this is a subject that is too frightening both for women and their need for security and for men and their need to protect and defend. To protect and defend one must have some thing and/or someone who needs defending. By inferring that God created all of humankind equal and endowed us each, male and female, with loving, caring, intelligent, discerning abilities shakes at the foundation of our cultural heritage which is based in our understanding of Scripture. To imply or to admit that we may have been wrong about something in which we have invested our life, calls for more pain than most of us are willing to endure. I believe that our interviews, our brainstorming and our groups show us that we have a long way to go on the journey and that many clergy, both female and male, are not willing to pack their bags. I, therefore, believe that we began with the greatest intention of covering the issue of justice as it relates to women in ministry, but we were not able to convey that as we intended because of the immediateness of the pain that the people in our groups were experiencing on a day-to-day basis. As Anne Wilson Schaef brought out in Women's Reality, "Somehow, we must begin to realize that the theology of our culture—White Male System theology—forces us into a static system of hierarchy and exploitation. We must begin to see how current theological assumptions serve to perpetuate the White Male System and limit human freedom and growth." [69] To paraphrase her, "We have begun."

Tom: It seems to me our theological rationale is the biblical witness has been utilized to degrade and dehumanize women for centuries, and what I have discovered in our Project is even today we still see injustice is done to those who are counted as marginalized people by the ones who are called by God to proclaim God's Word.

Leta: It has been made clear to me through this study that even though we say that we use Jesus the Christ as our model, whose very nature reached out to bring those outside the gate in, we as leaders in the Church have to find a rationale other than the Christ in order to do the same thing that he did.

Tom & Leta: It is our belief that our theological rationale is complete in its current state. We had hoped during our group meetings we would touch on some of our theological underpinnings, because it is very important to both of us. We find, however, either we were not able to interject it into the discussion or our participants did not find the theological to be as important to them as it was to us.

The book we chose for study was not oriented toward the theological. We made the error of presupposing that our people, all of whom were clergy persons, would employ their theological knowledge in interpreting the text and thus discuss it theologically in our groups. We now find that that is the basis on which we (you and I) do ministry through our preaching of the Word and our living out the Faith but that is not necessarily the way all others do it. We would, therefore, intentionally work it into the discussion if we were to undertake this Project again. It is our belief that in order to bring about valid change of any kind in both the clergy and lay community, it is vitally important that it have a recognized theological base. This theological base translates itself as biblical base. Both groups want to know "where it says that in the Bible." Scripture is one of the four theological groundings that we United Methodist pastors preach.

We feel good about our balance between our use of the Hebrew scriptures and the gospels found in the New Testament. Although no one in our groups brought up the Pauline writings, we perhaps would introduce them if we were to do the Project again just as we would emphasize the theological base of our Project. We realize it is the Pauline writings which have the most powerful effect on this issue of women's rights not only in the present day but in the day that formed most of the people who are members of this annual conference. For good or ill, the Hebrew scriptures are often simply written off as not as valid. Leta's experience in teaching "The Church in Solidarity With Women" validates the importance of resurrecting those stories and teaching them in a new light. When people are shocked to find that there is a portion of the Holy Scripture with which they are unfamiliar, they are most always open to change. We have found this is true of clergy as well as the laity. There are those, however, who say, "Let's leave the gory stories hidden. There might be a child in the audience."

Our personal bias toward Scripture as the foundation for our understanding of liberation probably was responsible for the fact that we did not bring any liberation theologians, male or female, or any women theologians into our theological discussion. This probably would have strengthened our discussion. We discussed it with each other, however, and felt that it was necessary to draw a boundary on this chapter, and the Scripture, particularly as it relates to the Christ, was the most relevant to our particular concern. The other theologians were not totally neglected but we felt them to be tangential to our particular concern. We did, however, bring theological discussion into our other chapters. Given our topic we could easily have introduced Ruether's thesis that, "This language in the Gospels belongs to the tradition that criticizes existing power systems and places God on the side of the oppressed."[70] Both the groups could have discussed the new revolutionary, transforming power where "...power (is) exercised through service, which empowers the disinherited and brings to all a new relationship of mutual enhancement."[71] This probably would have worked well with the female clergy but may have been seen as just another attempt by a radical feminist theologian to disrupt their lives.

We must not forget, however, the words of Brock in her sermon, "The courage to choose/the commitment to be chosen." In feminist reversals of patriarchal power, we look not to the famous and powerful for truth, but to the marginal, to the invisible and the unheroic courage we find in the lives of ordinary women and men" such as "...an unwed pregnant teenager whose son became a carpenter."[72]

Tom & Leta: As we reflect upon our theoretical assumptions, we would not change anything which we proposed was important to this project. We used a vast array of sources who approached the issues which we felt were important from different standpoints. The reading was exciting and inviting to anyone who has even a minimal interest in the issues of women and men in ministry. We used both male and female sources and interacted with the ideas presented therein.

Knowing that we would use Women's Growth in Connection in the action phase of our Project, we purposely did not use it as a major resource for our theoretical chapter. Looking back from this vantage point, we believe that it would have added to the breadth of our discussion had we used it, because our groups did not discuss it in as much detail as we had hoped they would. We could not have known that in the beginning. It speaks so powerfully to our problem that we mourn the fact that it does not enter into our theoretical chapter in a more meaningful way.

Our greatest problem in this theoretical chapter was in deciding which material to use. We read widely, and once we knew our emphasis, "everything" became useful to our Project. It seemed that every day someone had a book to recommend, the newspaper was full of articles and cartoons and the television programs became topics of analysis rather than comedy routines. We asked ourselves, "How could anybody be interested in anything other than this?"

Is there something that we would change or delete from our theoretical chapter if we had it to do over? The assumptions that we made were drawn from conscientious study of our sources and so we tend to want to say that this is as good as it gets. However, we realize there is always something that could be added that would make our study fuller and more well-rounded. What we would change has to do with our goal for our study. We originally stated that we hoped to make a significant change in the annual conference through our studying and discussing of the issues that relate to justice for female clergy. We stepped back from that hope to say that it is sufficient to believe that what we do matters. Had we kept with our original intention, we would have had some starting point for evaluating the effectiveness of our Project. As it is, we do not have anything that is tangible to evaluate. We still believe that what we have done matters, but we are at a loss to evaluate fully what our Project has accomplished. We do believe that we have been able to raise the consciousness of the persons in our study groups. They were not the same people who came into our groups. We have also seen change and growth in the four congregations we have served since beginning this Project together. We may never know the effect of what we have done except as we see it acted-out by these persons and by those whom they touch. This is, however, the nature of our ministry as well. For in ministry, we are never sure of the long-range effects of what we do or say. We continue in faith that some of what we do or what we say makes a difference in the lives of the people of God whom we serve. Now and then we see and hear it acted out by them.

Practicum Planning

Leta & Tom: We chose this Project because we believe that there is a definite problem throughout the Church, and specifically the United Methodist Church of which we both are part of its ordained clergy, involving abuse of power by men over women. We wanted to approach this from the standpoint of bringing justice to all those involved in one particular conference. This issue often involves the different ways that males and females communicate with one another and how they carry out ministry based on our own personal experience. We also chose to conduct two clergy groups running simultaneously, one male and one female, to discuss the book, Women's Growth in Connection, with the hope of awakening concern over the issue. In thinking about this from our present vantage point, we need to ask what we would change about what we proposed?

Tom: I believe that I have learned something of value which can be used in the continuing journey toward justice for women. The most important thing that I have learned has been that there is a great deal of ground work left to be done before any change can take place. I went into this project with the feeling that much of what we were going to present in our groups was not new or earth-shattering. Indeed, it was new and earth-shattering for the participants of my group. My group was not ready for the material presented. I think that we should have chosen a more basic book for our study material in order to familiarize the group members with the issues on a more simplistic level. I presupposed that the members of my group had been introduced to some of the ideas we talked about while in seminary as I had been or had possibly had some experiences that would have sensitized them to the plight of women in ministry. I should have remembered my own experience where it did not just rub off on me no matter how hard the female students at my seminary pled their case. What about you, Leta?

Leta: All the members of my group were well-informed as to the issues. With the exception of the one group member who never bought the book, they found the material exciting and were able to apply it to their own life experience, not only in ministry but in the secular world. Even the one who never bought the book responded and learned from the group discussion. They have all grown accustomed to the dehumanizing manner in which they are often treated not only by many of their male colleagues but by their parishioners, both male and female, as well. The study book gave them a tool which they can use to work within the system with a sense of integrity. The major issue as it relates to bringing about change whereby there can be a more just system is that there is very little fire left in those who participated. Neither do they see any other female clergy in their conference who is willing to enter into the struggle. In order to avoid pain, we women fall into the way of thinking described by Anne Wilson Schaef in <u>Women's Reality</u>.[73] In addition, there is fear not only of future hurt emotionally if they become involved but also of financial hurt because of loss of position if they become too involved in issues of women's rights. Heaven forbid that they be labeled a "feminist!"

Tom & Leta: It appears that part of our learning has been that the material we chose to study was appropriate for the group of female clergy but not necessarily for the group of male clergy. The women appeared to take to the material readily; whereas, the men balked at much of what was presented because they considered it to be too radical. Our Project emphasizes again the great difference between the male and female clergy in the conference which could say more than one thing. The women are open to learning about anything that can alleviate the pain that they experience in their ministry every day. The men, however, are fearful of learning anything new because the change that might take place would be a loss of power and certainly painful for them.[74] Most of us choose to get out of pain rather than to get into a journey that produces pain unless there is something in it for us. We had presupposed that there was something in it for the men, because we believe that the oppressor suffers in an oppressive situation as well as the oppressed. We have found that maybe this is not always true, or at least the suffering that the oppressor experiences is not always evident to them.

Critical Evaluation

As we reflect upon the design and planning of our Project, we hold as a good plan the idea of having two groups running simultaneously, one with an all-female clergy membership and one with an all-male clergy membership, using the same material for discussion. We found that the points brought up by each group separately for sharing within the entire group were amazingly alike, despite the wealth of ideas presented in the book used for discussion, but that the reactions to these ideas were very different. Because there were two groups, this method left us with some solid material rather than with generalizations about how males and females think and communicate differently about the same stated issues. It also supported our thesis which was that the different ways in which we communicate as male and female clergy persons makes all the difference in who is "successful" within the appointive system of the United Methodist Church because of who controls the power. The identity of those in our two groups remain anonymous to all but the two of us. The members of one group were never told the names of the participants of the other group. It is amazing how, even unplanned, their stories of ministry, both fulfilled and unfulfilled intertwined with one another.

In assessing the positives we found that meeting in the same room of a building in a central place for each session was helpful to provide continuity and comfort for these short-term groups. The people who were invited to be a part of these groups all knew each other, but some of them had only minimal knowledge of each other.

Another positive was the size of the groups. They were manageable and provided each group member ample time to voice their impressions of the readings and to discuss their varying viewpoints. The small size of the groups helped to foster intimacy which could not have been achieved in a larger group.

It is our opinion now that meeting once a week rather than every other week as we did would have been better even if we still limited it to six sessions. Something was lost in each interval. It was not possible to pick up where we left off, as was illustrated in Leta's group between session two and session three, although the intentions were extremely good. This was even harder to do when a group member missed a session and was thus away from the group for a month. It called for an entirely new beginning each time. To avoid such a situation in the future, our ideal would be to require a commitment to attendance. We had hoped that that issue would have been understood because of the excitement which the material evoked and because each of the participants chose to be part of the group.

If we had it to do over again, we would have more sessions than we did this time, and we would cover only one chapter during each session. We realize that we only skimmed the surface of most of the material and yet dealt with some of the material in great depth. The women in Leta's group were so very eager that she meet her educational goal, and voiced this commitment more than once, that they rejected the proposition intentionally to carry over discussing material from a prior session into a new session. Leta would have preferred a more   in-depth discussion of a few ideas rather than skimming a number of ideas and issues. It may not have occurred anyway. Was this nurturing of Leta or avoidance of an in-depth discussion on the part of the women to move on?

Another possibility for future groups would be to hold a weekend or a two to three day retreat based on the material used for the Project. There would be the added advantage of the community which always is created in retreat settings. It grows out of the eating and the sleeping and the playing together. In such a setting each meal time can then be Holy time. Leta sees that such a milieu would have enhanced the female clergy group, for they missed the breaking of bread together. Since the female group's meeting place was neutral to all of us, it would have been very difficult for one of us to prepare for such a sharing. Another impediment to this plan was the fact that all the clergy women were always on their way to work which issue was ever-present in their thinking.

This particular conference holds required workshops on racism and sexual harassment. It would appear from our study and experience that required workshop on bettering communication between male and female clergy persons is certainly as important as the above because of the injustice that now exists for female clergy in the Church.

It was good to have the great age range in our groups. We were able to see how differently the older group members of the female clergy group felt about certain issues as opposed to the younger ones. The oldest member of this group was very typical of her generation in her responses as she accepted a subservient role as "God's will;" whereas, the younger women were more willing to challenge male authority and the misuse of power both on theological and secular grounds. This could have been simply a difference in personality, but it also could have been due to the fact that her father and her husband, the two males closest to her, had always been supportive of her self-development as were those males in the life of the leader of the group.

In Tom's group he had hoped to see a striking difference between the older and the younger members because of the exposure of the younger clergy persons to women's issues, but he did not.

As far as leadership is concerned, Leta would be more aggressive in the presentation of the study material if she had it to do over again. As an experienced teacher and group leader, that has always proved to be successful for her. She is not positive, however, that this group of clergy women would have accepted that style of leadership. There seemed always to be an over-riding interest in the sharing of news from around the annual conference or in their individual parishes. That news took precedence over the topic at hand. The material to be covered was important to Leta, because she is more prone to confront injustice in her ministry, thus the choosing of this doctoral project. It is, however, her agenda and was not necessarily the agenda of this particular group.

Tom's leadership style was to make a conscious effort to allow the group to self-direct their conversations. Even though he brought a set of questions to the group meetings, he intended for these questions merely to be prompters to get the group discussing the issues brought forth in the book. The questions were helpful in keeping the group on task; however, the group was more than willing to discuss the book. He took on the role of facilitator in that he prompted and prodded the discussion, but the discussion was the central focus of the group, not his leadership. Upon reflection, he would not change this style of leadership.

Because we both would have preferred to have each group session based on the theological implications of the study and presupposed that the clergy persons invited to be in the group would want the same thing, we both would become more active in assuring that this would take place. For example, we would probably be intentional in having prayer and a short "thought for the day" to begin each session and a "sending-out" rather than looking at one's watch to decide that the session was over.

Any new group which we would form would be more of a covenant group style. This would entail certain boundaries being set as to a commitment of attendance in the sessions and to the faithful reading of the material. We are glad that we did limit the group to people who would commit to stay with the group on a regular basis rather than accepting those who wanted to come and go at their convenience although some members still treated it in that manner by their absences.

Two questions come to mind and perhaps could have impacted our Project in some way. The first has to do with written contact. It was made before and after all but the fourth and fifth sessions. Only one person showed up for the fourth session of the women's group and one for the fifth session of the men's group. Would a written notice have made any difference, and why, if the group or the study was important to them, did they need written reminders?

The second question has to do with the preparation of the group members for the sessions. Would it have been helpful to ask the members to prepare a set of questions from their reading of each chapter? Even though we discussed their questions and responses to the readings, this was not done immediately after they had read the material. Their first impressions had to be recalled rather than coming fresh from their exposure to the readings.

In our dialogue together at this point in our Project, we regret that we did not explore more fully an evaluative process to be used with the participants in the groups. As stated earlier, this was not a part of our Project because we had shifted our goal from one of effecting change in the annual conference to one of presenting the issues and then hoping that what we were saying and doing would matter. We still believe that what we are saying and doing matters; however, we believe that our Project might have a greater impact if there had been built in an opportunity for the group members to put into writing their reactions to the entire process rather than just voicing it at the end of the last session.

We both plan to initiate this study in other groups which we form or of which we are invited to become a part, because the problem of misuse of power by the male clergy in the Church is a serious one as is the disenchantment of female clergy with the existing hierarchical system from which they are effectively counted-out. If we can in any way bring about better communication, better dialogue and more meaningful study with one another so that all persons in ministry are treated justly and experience wholeness, then our Project will have accomplished its purpose.

The experience of conducting the study group and the research of this topic will be a part of who we are forever. The most important learning for us has been in the area of how males and females are fundamentally different in the way we relate to one another and in the manner in which we carry out tasks of ministry. We look at life from very different perspectives. It is this difference of perspective that we believe is a root cause for much of the miscommunication and consequently a cause of the injustice that is perpetrated against female clergy. Of course, we are not so naive as to believe that differing perspectives are the only cause of injustice, but our learning about these different perspectives has given us cause to understand those differences as one of the causes amidst a myriad of causes. We have both been moved to the forefront of a new liberation frontier, and we can say to God with great enthusiasm, "I know where you want me to stand today!"

Tom: What a transforming journey this has been for me! I thought that I was free of prejudice in all areas of my life. Some of my best friends were women clergy. I had never really given much thought to the struggle that women endure in order to gain even entrance into ordained ministry. Yes, I knew intellectually what some women had gone through in the process of ordination, but somehow it did not bother me. It was their problem—not mine.

As we come to the close of this part of the journey together, I return to my entrance into the United Methodist Church. I knew that the United Methodist Church ordained women and took them into full-connection, and, although the denomination from which I was coming did not do so, this did not pose a problem for me. It was all right with me that women were ordained and serving as ministers; however, I would not have wanted a woman for a pastor. Being ordained myself, I would not have to face that dilemma. I certainly was not rude to any of my female colleagues, and I thought that I treated them just as I did my male peers. I even began to respect one as a mentor with whom I had very close contact in a small group setting. I cannot pinpoint, as Paul did on the road to Damascus, the event that brought about my recognition that I was merely accepting women as colleagues to the intentional commitment that indeed there were women whom I would not only accept but seek out as my pastor.

I realize that I have been profoundly affected by this Project. I can no longer look at things the same way that I did before Leta and I began this journey together. I can no longer listen to abusive and derogatory language of colleagues and parishioners toward women clergy in particular, and women in general. It is much more than mere recognition of my life situation. It is a sense of urgency that I feel to learn more and to stand in solidarity with my sisters and my mothers in their struggle for wholeness. For as long as they do not experience wholeness, neither can I feel whole.

Leta: It is difficult to write a closing statement to a Project which has dominated my life for more than three years. Reading a book on any subject, reading the daily newspaper (See appendix 6), having a simple conversation became a part of my journey into understanding the hurts and confusion, even the despair, experienced by my female colleagues in ordained ministry. Many times I have been called to reflect upon my journey with my husband as he tried to open my eyes to the injustices toward women which our society and our church inflicts and which I wanted to ignore. No story which I have encountered during this period of time has reached beyond the realm of the credible.

Journeying with Tom has been a powerful part of my personal process. Tom cannot escape his environmental upbringing as part of the white male dominant class. As we have sat through interviews together, he has become aware of the fact that male interviewees have spoken only to him and treated me as invisible despite my age and my experience and the topic which we were discussing. As we have worked on scripture, he has been amazed at what had been invisible to him until I pointed it out to him. Dialoguing and struggling with him for hours on end has been painful but enriching. To see his growth as one reared to ignore the female when issues of power came on the scene, has given me hope. This experience has been part of the processing of the model for growth for me.

Three of my own stories, which took place during the preparation of this Project, will serve as closure to my part of this work. Their impact upon my life and my ministry will stay with me for a long, long time.

The first incident was the occasion of my preaching a sermon. A male clergy person was present who had power over my life in ministry. He remarked before a sizeable group of people who also had power over me that my sermon was a feminist sermon, that he hated feminists, that the sermon had nothing to do with the Gospel and would in fact destroy any church body to whom it was delivered. To the contrary, however, the response was good, and one elderly gentlemen, a retired judge, remarked that he had learned more and been changed more by that sermon than by any other which he could remember. I remembered the remark of the man in power, and I realized that I was not at all afraid of him. I was free. I did not argue with him. I simply pondered his statement in my heart.

The next event followed the delivery of the word that I had been approved for ordination. A person on the committee said something about our conference having much that needs changing and that the members of the committee were afraid that I would withdraw from the conference. I was totally confused. Why would I withdraw from a group into which I had struggled so hard to enter? It was later interpreted to me that what had really been said was, "Leta will buck the system." How could they have known that this statement was a compliment to my integrity rather than a slap of my hands? I knew with whom I needed to stand.

It was soon after this incident that I took this Project proposal to our Field Supervisor, a woman who is not a United Methodist and is not all that familiar with our system of pastoral appointment. When she read it, her eyes showed her delight. She then cautioned me that by carrying out this Project involving me in justice issues for women, I would endanger my appointment in the church. "Oh, no," I responded. "I've done an excellent job, and the people love me. My record of service is good." Within a few weeks after the word was out about the nature of my Project, the issue of respect raised its ugly head, and I was reappointed to a place where I would not be working directly under the supervision of a male pastor. Again, I knew with whom I needed to stand.

It was later, after I was serving in the place were I was reappointed that I was in a group of clergy persons laughing and having a good time. One of the male clergy persons who had not known me over a long period of time grew more serious. He mentioned that my reputation precedes me wherever I go. "You are known not only as self-confident but as overly self-confident—a challenge by most clergy persons as one to break down." How very strange to be seen as one to break rather than to grow with in ministry. Again, I knew with whom I needed to stand.

These were not someone else's stories. They were mine. If this could happen to me, it could happen to any woman and most likely would. Some of the women who were my colleagues did not have either the life experience or the respect of the lay women of the conference which I did. I knew that more harm could be done to me, but I also knew that God had made it clear to me a long, long time ago as I read to Grandma that I was to stand beside the marginalized and the oppressed, no matter the cost. This Project helps me to say, "Yes, Lord, I will stand beside the women who are written out of the Holy Family and most surely out of the places of ministerial leadership of our organized churches to which we refer as our church families." I will accept ownership of my own place among them as one who is marginalized and oppressed.

And, yet this is not the end of my story. My love for the Church is boundless; I would not have undertaken this Project if that were not so. It has been the center of my life since my birth. It was the place where I was formed as a loving, accepting person. It has been my shelter in the storms of life, my refuge in the midst of grief and pain. It is the place where I experience joy and laughter in the fullest sense of these words. It is where I draw strength to confront any form of evil done to humankind. As Brother Roger of Taize says,

> *When the church becomes a land of reconciliation,*
> *when she is maternal and welcoming for humanity,*
> *when the church is a land of simplicity then I think*
> *people come running from the ends of the earth to*
> *understand and to be there.*

Footnotes

69   Anne Wilson Schaef, Women's Reality, Third Edition. (San Francisco: HarperSanFrancisco, 1992), pp. 175-176.

70   Ibid., p. 30.

71   Ibid., p. 30.

72   Farmer, David Albert & Hunter, Edwina, eds., And Blessed Is She, Sermons by Women, (New York: Harper & Row Publishers, 1990) pp. 117-118.

73   We struggle desperately not to accept the awareness that men do not understand us completely because they cannot. They are able to understand little—if anything—beyond the pale of the White Male System unless they take special care to because they do not believe other systems exist. Ibid., p. 60.

74   This is because "superior " system people are often slow learners and are not very motivated to learn about other systems. Why should they? They're already in charge! Ibid., p. 60.